KITCHEN GARDENS OF FRANCE

Louisa Jones

Photography by Vincent Motte

THAMES AND HUDSON

CONTENTS

ABOVE : Dr Morère strawberry.

LEFT : French potagers are age-old, but can also be avant-garde.

FLYLEAF : Heirloom vegetables grown by Jean-Luc Danneyrolles.

FRONTISPIECE : Les Banlieusards, photo by Robert Doisneau.

A WORLD OF WONDERS

Twenty years ago, a young Parisian eyed my rather exuberant kitchen garden in southern France and commented, 'This is lovely. Do you have to do anything, or does it get like that all by itself?' Today few 'city slickers' would be so ignorant of country ways. Many are planting tomatoes themselves, if only on a balcony. The current vogue for vegetable gardening has changed many lives – how deeply, time will tell.

Today the potager or kitchen garden is high fashion, but the stylish version has its roots in centuries of down-to-earth, practical gardening. Its traditions have been maintained in every French region and by every class of society. The very word '*jardin*' long meant, to the vast majority of the French population, a kitchen garden. An official government survey recently claimed that twenty-three per cent of the fruit and vegetables consumed in France comes from family patches. The retired shopkeeper, the urban dentist, the 'back-to-the-land' idealist, the hospital administrator, the factory worker, the country postman, the civil servant, the television producer, the scientific researcher and the street-sweeper – all these and more may now be growing their own vegetables.

For scholars and historians, the formal *jardin à la française* has traditionally embodied the essence of French gardening. Some acknowledge the potager's importance but judge that this humbler mode 'belongs more to agriculture than horticulture'. Today, farming generally means something more extensive, uniform and even industrial. The kitchen garden – intimate and ever-changing – provides a much more personal field of endeavour, so to speak. At the same time, one much more typical of the French experience than the *jardin à la française*, as it is shared by people of all regions and origins.

Some contemporary French potagers are deliberately designed to be beautiful. Others achieve this unintentionally, simply by mingling herbs, fruit and flowers among the vegetables as has always been done in this country. English designer Gertrude Jekyll, the mother of modern horticulture, might have been writing about the French potager when she commented, 'The size of a garden has very little to do with its merit. It is merely an accident relating to the circumstances of the owner. It is the size of his heart and brain and goodwill that will make his garden either delightful or dull, as the case may be, and either leave it at the monotonous, dead level, or raise it, in whatever degree he may, towards that of a work of fine art'.

When I first began exploring the world of contemporary French vegetable gardens, I feared it would turn out to be just a fad – a modern version of Marie Antoinette's playing milkmaid. But the more I visited gardens all over the country, the more I realized that the current trend runs very deep. Not just an expression of nostalgia for France's particularly rich rural heritage, the contemporary potager is helping establish a new balance between city and country living.

At the same time, the kitchen plot offers a special opportunity to slow down and participate in the rhythms of natural processes. Growing vegetables more than any other kind of gardening means a daily presence, a constant attention to detail, an awareness of seasonal change. And if there is a particular pace, so there is also a special spirit of place. Every potager has its own type of soil, its microclimates, its distinctive setting – and its individual gardener. France is the most diverse country in western Europe, with regions that resemble England, Germany, Italy, Spain...and others quite unique.

The much celebrated French art of living – in cuisine as in everything else – depends on making the most of what is specific to each place and each individual. Few nations have put so much care into the local and artisanal production of food as the French.

The vast domain of French potagers held many surprises for me in my explorations. Tiny or tremendous, formal or romantic, makeshift or high-tech – its variety is quite astonishing. This is a sphere still very much on a human scale, made marvellous by 'the hearts and brains and goodwill' of the gardeners themselves. Dozens of them took time to show me their plots, eager to exchange garden gossip and comments on this year's weather – always unique, that too! I made many friends writing this book, and I would like to thank all of them for their warm welcome and for showing me – I who thought I already knew this world – how wonderfully diverse it truly remains.

LOUISA JONES, ARDÈCHE

Denis Brihat : Round Onion, partial gold toning.
PAGE 10 : Pumpkins piled for winter at the Château de Berzé.

I

HERITAGE GARDENS

Legend has it that the first French vegetable garden was dug by a medieval monk, St Fiacre. Allowed to keep whatever land he could reclaim from the wilderness between dawn and sunset, he miraculously cleared a vast plot. And when he sat on a stone to survey his creation, this improvised bench bore his imprint ever after.

Certainly succeeding centuries have carried his mark, for St Fiacre became the patron saint of gardeners. His influence has never been greater than today when, all over France, historic gardens are being restored and reconverted to new uses. Efforts are everywhere being made to re-create period potagers, and preserve a heritage now valued as never before. The magnificent gardens of Villandry are rightly celebrated world-wide, but the diversity of lesser-known potagers throughout the country is quite astonishing.

The reasons for this surge of enthusiasm are complex. One certainly is the orientation of serious historians in recent decades towards the study of everyday life, including the ways in which ordinary people fed themselves. The public has responded with enthusiasm – hence the success of the many 'ecomuseums' in all the provinces.

In many cases, the results of these efforts are strikingly beautiful, worth recording for that fact alone. But at the same time, there is often a fascinating human and social dimension to their revival. This is a tale not only of historical remains but of the ways in which different people, in all the provinces of France, experience them.

Potagers more than any other form of gardening are quickly made and quickly lost. To consider them in the light of history is to savour not only the pleasures of discovery but also those of an endlessly renewed creativity.

Monks and lovers

Medieval gardens have provided a major focus in the potager revival of the 1990s. Many striking architectural remnants find themselves thus provided with a colourful new setting without undue expense. These are not restorations, of course, but gardens created in a medieval spirit. But what exactly is meant by the medieval spirit? It has been variously interpreted to mean, first, a choice of vegetables cited by medieval sources and known to have been common before the Renaissance. The beautiful hyacinth bean with satiny purple-red pods (*Lablab purpureus* syn. *Dolichus lablab*), has had enormous success even in modern-style gardens.

At the same time, formal designs taking inspiration from manuscript illuminations feature woven wood fencing (called *fascines* or *plessis*) around raised beds of herbs, vegetables and flowers, with fruit trees, rustic arbours and grassy seats. These have such appeal that some professional garden designers have made up packages of instant medieval potagers, easy to put in place because of wooden structural features, but equally fast in their decay.

Inevitably there is much mystery about gardens evolving so long ago, and over a period of five or six centuries. However some documents have survived: a fourth- or fifth-century Gallic poem commends water running between the squares of a garden, dew shining on cabbage leaves and winsome roses. Only a few centuries later, the Merovingian Queen Ultrogotha, wife of Childebert, is portrayed by the Bishop of Poitiers in her gardens, probably in the Saint-Germain part of Paris, among green lawns, roses, vine-decked arbours and fruit trees grafted by the King himself, 'of suave scent and exquisite taste'.

No less than four precious documents have survived from the Carolingian period alone (late eighth and early ninth centuries). These are a list of plants (called the *Capitulare de villis vel curtis imperii*) to be grown on imperial lands which by then extended from the Netherlands to northern Spain and Italy, and from the Atlantic to Hungary; a detailed monastery plan proposed to the abbot of the influential monastery at St Gallen in present-day Switzerland; a charming short poem by Walafrid Strabo, a monk of the Benedictine abbey of

ABOVE : *Fifteenth-century gardeners sowing aromatic plants for use against the contagion of the Black Plague.*

LEFT : *Swede (Chou-rutabaga de Skirving, Vilmorin).*

Reichenau near St Gallen, describing a garden cultivated by his own hands; and a gardener's calendar by another monk, Wandelbert of Prüm. Historians suggest that the creators of these documents may have formed part of a wide and active circle around the court of Charlemagne, including the Abbot Benedict of Aniane in Languedoc and Alcuin of York, Bishop of Tours, who are known to have exchanged seeds. The latter has recorded his love for gardens where '... apple boughs smell sweetly, and white lilies are mingled with little red roses'.

Later sources about medieval gardens include illuminations, tapestries, and the whole body of courtly texts from Arthurian romance and the *Roman de la Rose*, culminating in a particularly influential work on the art of gardens by Pietro de' Crescenzi of Bologna, written in 1305 and much reproduced throughout the fourteenth and fifteenth centuries.

This body of material inevitably leaves gaps, and there are several controversies among experts. The presence of boxwood, for example: one museum curator protests energetically that the box edging surrounding raised beds of vegetables is an anachronism since it is an introduction of the Renaissance. Other scholars point out that box was a mainstay of Roman gardens and much appreciated in medieval times for its medicinal and magic properties, such as warding off storms. But was it used as an edging plant, or only as a herb, topiary or hedging?

A popular vision imagines all vegetables, medicinal plants, flowers and fruit happily coexisting in the cloisters of monasteries. Dr John Harvey, writing in *The Oxford Companion to Gardens*, states unequivocally that there is no evidence of anything more than grass in cloister plantings. Surely indeed most monasteries needed more produce than the space within the average cloister could be expected to produce? The St Gallen plan, meant for a particularly prosperous community, proposes a large kitchen garden by the poultry yards, an infirmary (herb) garden by the house of the resident physician, ornamental orchards doubling as a cemetery and a separate cutting garden, all of generous proportions. Its cloister plantings were grassy plots cut by paths in a Latin cross with, at their intersection, a stand of tall junipers shaped like a St Andrew's cross.

The four basic elements – vegetables, fruit, flowers and herbs – are cited by all sources as being present in medieval gardens, but the combination in which they were found is less clear. Confusion is fed by the fact that the basic categories were not then defined as they are now. The imperial list has two sections: fruit trees and herbs, but the latter include salads and pot-herbs, root vegetables such as carrot, parsnip, skirret, onion, and also such plants as madder and teasel. Jack Goodey, author of *The Culture of Flowers*, cites another list at Cluny from the end of the eleventh century where the poppy, lily and rose are listed under the category 'vegetables' (*olera*) as distinct from the leguminous plants. The St Gallen medicinal garden includes fennel, lovage (*Levisticum officinale*), lilies, roses, and flag iris, broad and haricot beans. Its vegetable list mentions celery and dill, poppies, parsley, chervil and 'gitto nigelle' described as a kind of black cumin. Savory was proposed for both plots.

No doubt there are no firm answers to these perplexities. But it is clear that by the twelfth and thirteenth centuries, two sorts of gardens appear over and over again: the *courtil* or *herbularium*, inside castle walls, meant often to be seen from windows above and consisting largely of a 'flowery mead' (*pré fleuri*), and the enchanted orchard (*viridarium* or *virgultum*) of larger proportions, outside the dwelling. Fishponds and aviaries commonly appear in the most ambitious ones.

The orchard, where lovers regularly took refuge, was fragrant with aromatic plants and full of flowers. Did vegetables belong to this aristocratic vision? A fifteenth-century Italian peasant caught stealing peaches was told to stick with 'the fruit of his equals' listed as turnips, garlic, leeks, onions and

shallots. But the highly influential, late fifteenth-century *Hypnerotomachia Poliphili* (The Dream of Poliphilo) conjures up a 'flowery mead' composed of 'all medicinal herbs' plus, quite explicitly, 'those which serve as food, that is to say cabbage, lettuce...' The long list includes asparagus, artichokes, peas and cucumbers. Root vegetables were always lower in the spiritual hierarchy than leafy ones. It is certainly true that there was not as yet a separation between utilitarian plants and ornamentals, and that medieval gardens appealed to other senses, notably smell and taste, as much as to the eye.

Historians posit also that, by the twelfth century, both the gardens of the aristocracy and larger monasteries carried on business as seedsmen and nurserymen, nuns being perhaps even more enthusiastic in plant production than monks. The presence of a commercial gardening trade by the thirteenth century is evidenced by the Parisian Guild charters. The different corporations have been described as *courtilliers* for courtyard gardens or *courtils*; *préoliers* specializing in meadows; *verdiers* or orchard gardeners; *treillageurs* for trellises and arbours; *maraîchers* who cultivated vegetables, often on marshlands; and *floresses*, usually women, who grew flowers. By the thirteenth and fourteenth centuries, the town gardens of *bourgeois* families or burghers were also expanding, and these definitely included vegetables.

Youth and joy at the Domaine du Villard in the Lozère

Medieval gardens imagined today by garden designers intermingle all vegetables, fruit, flowers and herbs, courtly orchards, flowery meads and potagers with happy abandon. Those created by scholars around historical monuments are necessarily more cautious but often just as beautiful – the courtyard of the Musée de l'Oeuvre in Strasbourg to cite but one example. Much more rare are attempts to re-create period potagers of common farms. A particularly delightful venture is the Domaine du Villard, set in the remote Massif Central department of the Lozère.

The Domaine occupies a satisfyingly picturesque knoll, in a fortified village, the apex of which is a fourteenth-century stronghold (Villard-le-Vieux). The more rustic Villard-le-Jeune grew up as a lay community at the foot of the castle at a time when the latter's fortifications housed a Benedictine community. Today it belongs to the commune of Chanac-Le-Villard and is administered by L'Association du Festival de Mende et du Gévaudan. Its high walls encircle ten massive limestone buildings with heavy roofs made of stone slabs over vaults, with a separate bread oven and dovecote. Its vast inner courtyards include a threshing floor, a medicinal garden and a vegetable garden. No mere museum, this complex now shelters active craft workshops, medieval banquets and merry festivals.

The potager at Le Villard is an imaginative reconstitution of a rustic garden, within battlements, on limited space. It is

RIGHT : Medieval manuscripts show vegetable beds enclosed in woven wood fencing. At Le Villard, laburnum branches are held in place with chestnut stakes.

FAR RIGHT : The farm buildings at Le Villard still have beautiful roofs of thin stone slabs (lauzes) . Today they house workshops teaching medieval crafts.

known that vegetables were originally grown on this spot, which can remain frost free even when other parts of the domain are frozen – the medicinal garden, for example.

The potager's large rectangle, entered through a high gate, is at a lower level than the stables above. It is designed very much as a pleasure garden as well as for productivity. The vegetable beds are here outlined with woven laburnum branches held in place with chestnut stakes. A simple wooden kiosk with a thatched roof rises in the very centre – an aviary (one of several at Le Villard). There is a small duck pond with a pair of mallards, and a few beehives. On the other side, a hornbeam bower shelters a welcoming bench. Over eighty

rosebushes, all varieties known to have existed before the Renaissance, thrive throughout. Some are useful to give the gardener early warning signs about powdery mildew in hot weather.

Against the walls grow commonly known plants – figs, apricots and vines in the most sheltered corners, hazelnuts and lilacs, peonies and mock orange elsewhere. Rhubarb arrived unannounced in one spot but, although anach-ronistic, has remained because the staff like to eat it. Its pres-ence bears witness to the good-humoured spirit of a place run by an enthusiastic and youthful team. The twenty-two-year-old gardener, Pierre Julia, is keen to improve his skills and has attended workshops at the horticultural schools in Grasse and Uzès.

Beyond the potager is a series of stables and pens for farm animals, varieties approximating as closely as possible to those common in the region in medieval times. As with vegetables, the animals tend to be smaller and hardier than their modern counterparts – the Jersey cow, for example, which used to be taken on long sea voyages – or hairy black pigs from Corsica. Gallic chickens are also small but lively, and ponies look similar in size to medieval horses. Guides remind visitors that mounted knights had to bend their knees to avoid dragging their feet on the ground.

There are also many beautiful types of pheasants and peacocks which used to be eaten at festive meals before the introduction of the turkey.

The princess of this magic estate is Anne Trémolet de Villers, who trained as an archaeologist. Author of numerous booklets on local history and sites, including a study of fifteen local troubadours, Anne first created the Festival de Mende in 1982 and ever since has set up the well-documented annual exhibits which enliven the Domaine. It is she who organizes digs, restoration work and the visits with unflagging energy (in spite of having five children at home). Her activities provide an intelligent model for the kind of cultural tourism which many historical monuments seek to promote, though too many get bogged down in the quicksands of bureaucracy.

The team Anne has formed at Le Villard consists of twelve permanent employees, only three of whom are over twenty-five years of age. It might be said, indeed, that the courtly virtues sung by troubadour poets – youth, joy and generosity – are still alive and well at Le Villard. And indeed in this remote mountain region, famous for sudden killing blizzards called 'tourmentes de neige', Le Villard evokes the lines of troubadour Bernart de Ventadorn: 'The ice I see is a flower, the snow, green things that grow'.

ABOVE : An aviary with a straw roof stands empty for the moment. The gardener setting out new leeks can enjoy the birdsong of free-flying companions.

LEFT : Colourful beds of cabbage and root vegetables surround a standard rose at the heart of the garden.

Battlements at the Château de Berzé in Burgundy

The Mâcon region of Burgundy is the heart of the country: everything here is at its richest and best. Lush pastures fatten up the famous white beef cattle, the Charolais, next to vineyards producing wines which Curnonksy called 'magnificent, powerfully fragrant'. Here the Romantic poet Lamartine spent his childhood and wrote some of his most celebrated works. From here, in medieval times, the abbots of Cluny ruled over a vast empire of Benedictine monasteries throughout Europe.

Many exceptional vestiges remain. At Berzé-la-Ville, where the Cluny abbots had a country house, a chapel contains rare murals. Nearby, the fortified castle at Berzé-le-Châtel with its forest of turrets and three rings of ramparts dominates the highway winding though the wooded valley below. Built to stand guard over the southern approaches to Cluny, it remains today the largest and best preserved château of the region. It

Formal gardens surround the living quarters of Berzé's medieval stronghold, while its vast kitchen garden occupies the lowest terrace – a long way down for a sprig of parsley.

ABOVE : *At Berzé, the imposing topiary towers date from the turn of the last century.*

RIGHT : *In this rich Burgundian valley, Charolais cows graze on the opposite hillside, beyond the lush, well-ordered vegetable rows.*

now belongs to the Comte and Comtesse de Milly, old Burgundian nobility, whose ancestors began its restoration in the nineteenth and early twentieth centuries. They also redesigned the gardens and added ranks of fat topiary chessmen at the entrance. All the green strips here stretch behind high battlements. The lowest and broadest terrace still contained within the castle walls is the potager.

North meets south at Berzé in the architecture, but also in the garden layout. Some high turrets are covered with dark, thin slabs of slate called *laves* in this region (*lauzes* in the centre of France) whereas the outbuildings have low-pitched, red-tiled, southern-style roofing. The walls are predominantly golden, but flecked with as many as seven different types of stone, some from as far north as Belgium, others from the south. And if the spacious potager is walled, like those of northern châteaux, at the same time its terrace lies like an open drawer, clearly visible from above like those of Mediterranean hillsides. Any potager with such a spectacular setting must of necessity be ornamental as well as productive.

The man who makes all this possible is the Portuguese gardener, Joachim de Costa. He has been employed at Berzé since 1969, when he came as butler and chauffeur for the old Count. He spent much time with his predecessor, a local man, and learned from him not only the cultivation of vegetables but the important process of winemaking, which is still the château's major activity (red Mâcon supérieur and Saint-Véran are sold on the property). Joachim became gardener himself when the old man retired. Now he maintains single-handed a park which requires much intensive care — the pruning of topiary and parterres, the management of fruit and wine production and the kitchen garden.

As everywhere, the vegetable mosaic evolves month by month, year by year. The design here is anchored however by certain permanent features, such as a hedged oval of grass around a small pond, outlined each spring by oleanders which are kept potted indoors in winter. Even more striking is the broad, wrought-iron gloriette set in the outer wall, and draped with wisteria. There are also rows of small fruit bushes tucked against the castle wall between the taller forms of free-standing

fruit trees; and along some vegetable beds, ancient, gnarled fruit cordons which the gardener managed to renew when everyone thought they had gone for good. Along the low, outer wall runs a line of rhubarb behind a severely clipped hedge. Finally, in the shelter of the massive north-western tower, rests a weathered well-proportioned greenhouse of comfortable appeal. In this refuge Joachim grows lemon and grapefruit trees in pots to provide cheerful summer décor among the vegetables but also as reminders of his distant Portuguese childhood.

Such is the framework within which rows and rectangles of vegetables expand and decline in everchanging patterns, their lines sometimes following the curve of the terrace, sometimes stretching at right angles to the battlements which protect the garden, at least in part, from drying west winds. All is colour and profusion. Joachim obviously enjoys experimenting with the looks of things, planting a carpet of strawberries at the foot of the old fruit trees, or setting stripes of copper-toned batavias, puce curly endive and red cabbages together in a cold frame. Indeed plantings may be made deliberately for display rather than need – witness the 950 Bleu de Solaize leeks, with their characteristic metallic tone, set out like a regiment on parade. Nor does this artist disdain the simple seduction of well-tilled, rich brown earth, lying like a parchment ready for the scribe. Aromatics such as parsley, tarragon, lemon verbena, chives, thyme and rosemary everywhere

intermingle with the vegetables, fruit and flowers as part of a woven tapestry, not each in its separate place.

Joachim is much appreciated by the present Count and Countess. When during a stroll round the garden, he bends suddenly and digs into the soil, they follow suit – all three scrambling to dig up ant eggs which Joachim slips into an old seed packet. These are a treat for Joachim's tame pheasant, who goes by the name of Turbot because it moves like a fish. Much easy banter passes back and forth about this unusual pet.

The Count and Countess winter in Paris and are happy to know the property is in such capable hands in their absence. Still, if the Countess should bring vegetable seeds from far-distant Paris, Joachim wonders at the crazy ideas of city-dwellers. How can seeds from Paris be expected to grow in Burgundy? It is an old story: the newly converted city gardener wants to experiment, the old-timers remain as firmly rooted in tradition as their ancient fruit cordons. At Berzé, however, the dialogue must nonetheless be successful for the gardens are thriving. In 1992, they were opened for visits in July and August for the first time.

Perhaps the château's many varieties of cabbage now serve for the preparation of stewed partridge *à la mode de Cluny*, one of the Burgundian regional dishes appreciated by the gastronome Curnonsky. And perhaps in the thirteenth century, an abbot of Cluny was already entertained with a similar dish with cabbage grown, already then, in the potager of Berzé-le-Châtel.

ABOVE: Joachim de Costa, once chauffeur, now gardener, makes the Berzé garden thrive.

LEFT: Provincial style in French potagers always involves characteristic regional architecture, nowhere more strikingly than in this Burgundian bastion.

LA MAISON DES CHAMPS DE PIERRE CORNEILLE

The country house of Pierre Corneille is an island of greenery in a lunar industrial landscape south-west of Rouen. To pass within its walls is to enter a time machine. Here, the Corneille family lived for some years from 1639. Today the museum's imaginative curator, Evelyne Poirel, has created a period potager and orchard, where four main beds and nine smaller squares brim over with vegetables, herbs and flowers. Madame Poirel consults La Quintinye when in doubt but wonders about some of his notes. What, for example, did he mean by a 'sad geranium'?

The museum evokes the concrete, everyday life of a great author – a man who lay abed late, for example, when in need of inspiration. The bread oven, orchard, well, barn and woodyard which existed in his time suggest a life of order and rustic harmony.

The presence of the past

The transition from medieval to Renaissance gardening in France is another subject of scholarly debate: was Italian influence preponderant or was there a direct indigenous evolution from medieval to modern? Those who value progress towards the intellectual geometries of neo-classical gardens such as Versailles dismiss early sixteenth-century French examples as incoherent because their esplanades show no clear hierarchy either among the levels or with respect to the buildings. This line of argument praises the artistic superiority of Italian conceptions because of the internal order which they gradually impose. Progress towards the grandeur of Versailles entails also, over time, a clear separation between utilitarian and ornamental sections so that potagers and orchards, while still much valued, become separate entities, set apart from the main parterres.

A more recent trend in garden history, hotly argued by Denise and Jean-Pierre Le Dantec in their admirable *Roman des jardins de France*, admires and defends designs which prefer sensuality over rationality, admitting internal 'disorder' as proof of exuberance and vitality. The Renaissance châteaux gardens are seen as prolonging the French medieval aesthetic in which gardens exist for all the senses at once, not for purely visual or conceptual pleasure. Rabelais provides the model for a French tradition celebrating creation in all its parts, all the more so if these are irrationally ordered. Potagers and orchards belong right in the heart of such gardens.

The gardens of many French sixteenth-century Renaissance châteaux, including several famous Loire valley sites, are known to us largely through the engravings of Jacques Androuet du Cerceau. Published in 1576 and 1579, these drawings in our century directly inspired Dr Joachim Carvallo, owner and creator of the famous gardens at Villandry. Most have three tiers

ABOVE : *Work in the garden in April; early seventeenth-century engraving.*
LEFT : *Large Green Paris Artichoke (* Gros vert de Laon, *Vilmorin).*

of flat terraces as at Villandry, and often, as there, the lowest level is composed of a vegetable parterre. Such gardens do already operate a separation of sorts. While the potager still forms a major part of the display, admired from all angles, it nonetheless occupies the lowest level of a garden constructed around a symbolic movement upwards from earthy appetite to parterres representing forms of courtly love, and thence to the topmost green and water garden, dedicated to the spirit or soul. This symbolism, typical of the Renaissance, was particularly cherished by Dr Carvallo, who had recently converted to Catholicism when he created the gardens at

Villandry. But it is said that he preferred the potager, as most people do today.

Another Renaissance inspiration is the southern gardener Olivier de Serres, generally recognized as the father of French agronomy thanks to his influential *Théâtre d'agriculture et mesnage des champs* (first published in 1600). He experimented in a modest plot of less than an half a hectare at the Domaine du Pradel in the Vivarais. Few figures in the history of French gardening have as much appeal as this man, who, in amiable partnership with his wife, created an island of tolerance in a time of pitiless religious wars, improved the lot of thousands with his promotion of the silk industry through the planting of mulberry trees, and introduced many new varieties of food-producing plants.

Serres' writing is ever practical, obviously based on personal experience, full of delight and even humour. But in the garden he enlarged after 1600, he too separated the pleasure garden from its utilitarian counterpart, even if the latter was perhaps even more important than the former in his projects for domestic felicity. They co-exist, side by side, although Serres lets food plants cross the boundary, bordering his flower beds '*en lieu soileillant*' (on the sunny side) with strawberries 'which must be coaxed to remain in their dwelling'. Nonetheless, by his time the separation between useful and ornamental gardens has begun to be explicit and will grow ever greater through to modern times.

Cardinal Richelieu, in his wisdom, had Le Pradel razed and Serres' library destroyed. But less than a century after Serres' death, Jean-Baptiste de La Quintinye, vegetable gardener for Louis XIV, wrote his *Instructions pour les jardins fruitiers et potagers*. Published posthumously in 1690, it is full of excellent practical advice on vegetable gardening still generally relevant today. It was translated into English in 1693 by John Evelyn under the title *The Compleat Gard'ner*, and like the works of Olivier de Serres, deserves a modern edition.

Much of La Quintinye's energy was devoted to providing the ultimate luxury of vegetables and fruit out of their normal season. Orangeries and conservatories replaced the leafy constructions of earlier centuries. A Dutch visitor to Versailles in the early years decried the expense required to produce early peas for the royal table, a sentiment echoed later by Madame de Maintenon. It was assumed that natural law could be understood and therefore mastered and that the art of the gardener must therefore consist, in the potager as elsewhere, in manipulating it. Olivier de Serres had already advocated the use of glass bells to protect melons in autumn, but now the Orangerie provided shelter for palms, oleanders, olives, carob trees, figs, lemons and some two thousand orange trees.

Garden historians agree that the seventeenth century witnessed the triumph of mind over nature, though there are differing opinions about the place still occupied by fantasy and sensuality. The poet Malherbe wrote a famous homage, often quoted, to 'the most worthy king of the Universe who makes Nature yield to the miracles of Art'. Rigorous subordination of parts to the whole now meant, at the same time, a strict separation of genres in gardening as in literature. At Versailles, the Potager du Roi (still extant) was much admired by the Sun King but kept completely distinct from the main gardens. Thus the château potager has remained, in most cases, until the present day.

More and more French châteaux today have elaborate potagers, most of which are open to the public. Cynics may suggest that owners who meet with difficulty the enormous expenses of maintaining such properties can plant a potager much faster and more cheaply than a box parterre with an eye to drawing summer tourists as well as subsidies – perhaps a fair strategy, since the public, in France as in England, shows an increasing interest in vegetables. The columnist Tradescant in the Royal Horticultural Society's journal drew the wrath of the management at Glyndebourne opera one year when he suggested its décor of cabbages and courgettes had been planted only to fulfill a similarly urgent need for fast, cheap display, but he was criticizing the lack of coherent design, not the vegetables. Certainly the contrast between green geometries or old trees which seem eternally present and the mixed colours and textures of a potager as it evolves through a single season can charm owners and visitors alike.

If Villandry continues to draw admirers from all over the world, the French today often prefer more intimate examples such as the delicious walled garden of the Château de Miromesnil in Normandy (birthplace of Guy de Maupassant). Above all, the Château de Saint-Jean-de-Beauregard southwest

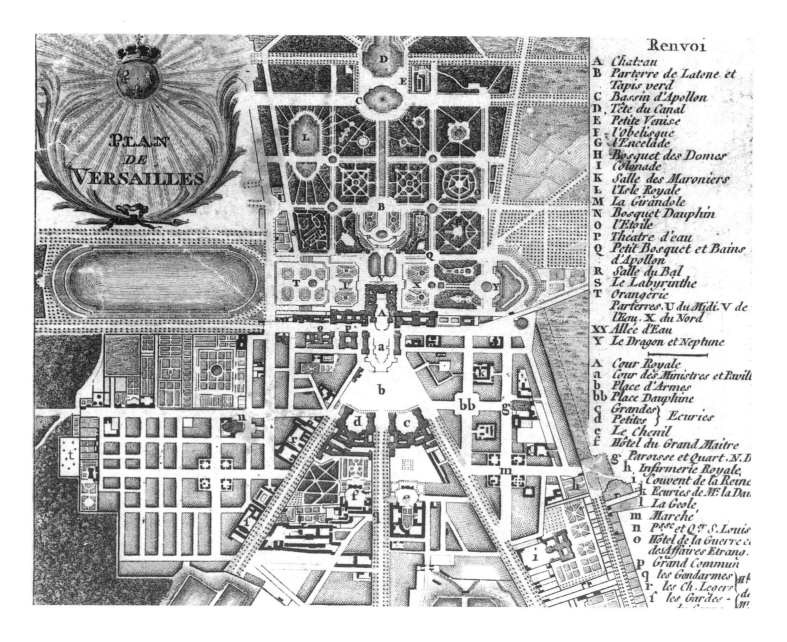

PLAN DE VERSAILLES

Renvoi

A Château
B Parterre de Latone et Tapis verd
C Bassin d'Apollon
D Tête du Canal
E Petite Venise
F l'Obelisque
G l'Encelade
H Bosquet des Domes
I Colonade
K Salle des Maroniers
L l'Isle Royale
M La Girandole
N Bosquet Dauphin
O l'Etoile
P Theatre d'eau
Q Petit Bosquet et Bains d'Apollon
R Salle du Bal
S Le Labyrinthe
T Orangerie
   Parterres. U du Midi. V de l'Eau. X du Nord
XX Allée d'Eau
Y Le Dragon et Neptune

A Cour Royale
a Cour des Ministres et Pavill
b Place d'Armes
bb Place Dauphine
c Grandes ⎫ Ecuries
d Petites ⎭
e Le Chenil
f Hôtel du Grand Maitre
g Paroisse et Quart. N.D
h Infirmerie Royale
i Couvent de la Reine
k Ecuries de M.ᵉ la Dau
l La Geôle
m Marché
n P.ˢˢᵉ et Q.ʳ S. Louis
o Hôtel de la Guerre et des Affaires Etrang.
p Grand Commun
q les Gendarmes
r les Ch. Legers
f les Gardes -

of Paris has come to symbolize the new potager image in a château setting. Its energetic owner, Muriel de Curel, has spared no effort to enhance her domain, where fashionable plant fairs are now held biannually (for perennials in April, fruit and vegetables in November).

Plan of the gardens of Versailles, whose king made 'Nature yield to the miracles of Art'. The Potager du Roi occupies the small squares in the lower left of the plan, just below the oval Pièce d'Eau des Suisses.

Ebony towers: the Château Dauphin and the Château d'Opme in the Auvergne

The Auvergne is a sombre, compelling province full of dark, coniferous forests clothing extinct volcanoes. Its narrow valleys once channelled streams of medieval pilgrims towards Italy or Spain, providing in every mountain hamlet Romanesque churches of breathtaking beauty. Their stonework makes good use of black volcanic basalt to create decorative patterns. Medieval châteaux were sometimes constructed entirely in this forbidding medium, tall fortresses rising from rolling terrain, affording hawk's eye views of the surrounding countryside. Two such dramatic bastions survive near the busy city of Clermont-Ferrand, the Château Dauphin twenty-two kilometres to the west at

ABOVE: A watering trough at the Château Dauphin in the dark volcanic stone of the Auvergne.

RIGHT: These impressive stone walls, admired by Montaigne, protect orderly beds of vegetables in plots now let to people from the village.

Pontgibaud, and the Château d'Opme (pronounced 'dom') nine kilometres to the south, in Romagnat.

Both date from the twelfth century and have kept their fortified aspect in spite of later transformations. Both stand on the edge of villages in the lives of which they play an important role. Both have terraced, Renaissance gardens spreading from the foot of the castle. In both cases, the most important element of the garden design is the potager, whose walls protect and yet leave open vast vistas beyond.

The Château Dauphin belongs still to the family which has owned it for 250 years, the Comte and Comtesse de Germiny. The Chateau d'Opme was purchased in 1989 by Monsieur and Madame Durin. Monsieur Durin grew up nearby, and remembers being invited to play there as a child of nine. These two ownerships contrast in a striking manner the fate of such old domains today – the first accomplishing a long, slow restoration, dependent largely on the bounties of the Caisse Nationale des Monuments Historiques; the second, thanks to private means, able to re-create in record time an elegant replica of former grandeur.

The potager of the Château Dauphin is unique. First of all, it is a sunken garden, on broad terraces surrounded by beautifully fitted, dark basalt walls on three sides, a disposition which creates not only protected microclimates but also striking visual rhythms. These must indeed have impressed essayist Michel de Montaigne who stopped there on his return from Italy in 1581. His visit may have been inspired by Du Cerceau, whose seminal work, published just before Montaigne's journey, included a drawing of these very gardens. For that reason, before embarking on the gardens at Villandry, Dr Carvallo also came to Pontgibaud to see them.

In a part of his diaries containing very little description, Montaigne devotes an entire paragraph to this visit: 'The small, rectangular garden is reached by raised paths four to five feet high. The beds below contain many fruit trees but

A previous generation restored the Château Dauphin around 1900. Today's family is concentrating on the gardens.

few pot-herbs and lie sunken between walls of cut stone'. It is perhaps not astonishing that the garden was bare at that time since Montaigne arrived on the ninth of November and, as he also reveals, 'there was so much snow, such a bitter cold wind, that one could see nothing of the countryside'. It is true that Pontgibaud, lying just over the crest of the Puy du Dôme, sometimes has hoarfrost as early as August. In summer, however, great stands of lupins at the foot of the battlements light up the tower behind, while repeating its shape and even, in the detailing of their flowers, the patterns of its masonry.

The gardens may not have changed much since Montaigne's time, though today their spread of a hectare on four levels is given over more to vegetables than to fruit. Two round basins have survived in good condition and provide water, piped from several kilometres away. Generous plots are now let for kitchen gardens to villagers for the modest sum of eighty francs a year but there are few demands, and not all the gardeners make the effort required for beauty as well as productivity. The Germinys, both recently retired, now live here all year round and have great hopes for extensive restoration to include an ornamental parterre by the great tower, a small 'English style' wood and a shrub border. But the garden's heart will remain its potager. Until funds can be gathered and plans confirmed, the Countess continues to mow the grass paths herself, and show visitors round the sumptuous collections of family mementos and furniture contained in the high rooms of the château. There are also full time caretakers who have lived next door for many years, and the two couples work hand in hand to keep the place going.

The Château Dauphin's potager has both historic significance and aesthetic promise, and if its restoration proceeds, it may become one of the most unusual examples in the country. Visitors open-minded enough to tolerate church bells will then be able to appreciate both its similarities with the Château d'Opme, also rooted in strong regional characteristics, and the differences of history, circumstance, and taste which mean that each has very much its own style.

The gardens of the Château d'Opme were laid out by Antoine de Ribeyre from 1613. His parallel avenues of limes still flank a broad basin and formal parterre at the foot of the castle, incorporating medieval ramparts into the composition. From this level, a twin-ramped formal staircase descends to the potager below, the design of which can thus be admired from above. A period orangery has survived built into this wall, between the two flights of steps.

Until 1992, the potager was abandoned to dense thickets of brambles, but under all this survived a cross outlined in box, and an astonishing fountain. Dating from 1617, it consists of standing naiads from whose breasts spouts not the milk but the water of life. This Mannerist motif was inspired by the designs of ... Jacques Androuet du Cerceau.

At the Château d'Opme (pronounced 'dom'), this amazing early seventeenth-century fountain stands at the heart of the potager. Here as at Villandry, vegetables are grown on the lowest terrace.

ABOVE : Cabbage, tomatoes, chard and Lollo Rosso lettuce provide contrasting colours and textures at the Château d'Opme. The challenge is how to harvest without destroying the design.

RIGHT : Four grass circles provide rest for the eye in this elaborate composition.

Was this level originally given over to the growing of vegetables? Oral tradition would have it that a potager always occupied this site. Its emplacement on a terrace below the formal parterre fits the usual pattern. The presence of walls and tall trees planted to break the force of the west wind would also confirm this interpretation. The south-east corner remains open on to one of those shimmering, seemingly infinite Auvergne views over volcanic summits, here looking out to the valley of the Allier.

The dark fountain stands today at the centre of four fan-shaped vegetable beds, each spreading around a simple circle of grass. Wisdom here lies in knowing when to leave such repose for the eye amidst the intricate patterns of red- and green-leafed salads, leeks, cabbages and other vegetables, all planted in concentric lines, the tallest along the outside edge, the lowest in the centre.

The Durins, with the help of Tonio, the old gardener whose fervour for the garden matches theirs, manage to pick lettuce without disturbing the design by choosing only every second one, and never taking two green or

two red ones at any one time. Along three sides, long borders of medicinal plants add colour with repeated groupings of golden achillea, dusky blue perovskia and catnip, and the white and yellow daisies of feverfew. Like the vegetable beds, these are outlined with dwarf box – some three thousand of these were planted in the early stages of the restoration.

Much character derives here not only from the pleasing patterns imagined by the present owners but also from the contrast between inky stone and soft, light, free-flowing vegetation. On the upper level, an immense, feathery gleditsia perfectly complements the sombre façade of the château. On top of the potager wall, Monsieur Durin has aligned dark stone pots spilling over with multicoloured sedums. And here as at the Château Dauphin, wonderful lichens in gold, green and orange find their way into the most secret corners.

These gardens lie behind a tall gate giving on to the main street of the village, and are invisible from without. But more and more visitors are discovering that the Château d'Opme's potager is among the best of the many restorations undertaken today around provincial châteaux.

RIGHT : Ripening pumpkins and purple perovskia.

FAR RIGHT : The paths here are made with puzzolane stone.

Peas and pirates: the Malouinière du Bos in Brittany

Country châteaux continued to imitate Versailles and Parisian models into the eighteenth century, even in such independent regions as Brittany. This province needs no introduction as a producer of fine vegetables. One of its best strips of fertile land lies west of Mont-Saint-Michel, towards Saint-Malo, a region which supplies two-thirds of the new potatoes eaten in France. Here a deep inlet called La Rance penetrates southward, still subject to tides although protected from chilling salt breezes. Nineteenth-century Romantic writer Chateaubriand describes this privileged country, called the Clos Poulet, as 'a continual mix of rocks and greenery, beaches and forest, creeks and hamlets' and adds that here 'every peasant, sailor and working man owns a small white house with a garden: among the pot-herbs, the

ABOVE : The Malouinières of Brittany were built for family living in the eighteenth century, and still fulfil this role perfectly.

RIGHT : New potatoes and peas – Breton specialities.

gooseberry and rose bushes, the iris and the marigolds can always be found a tea cutting from Cayenne, a tobacco plant from Virginia or a flower from China – some souvenir from another coast and another climate'. Indeed, from the eighteenth century, tobacco was grown commercially in the Clos Poulet, replaced only since World War II by artichokes, cauliflowers and potatoes.

The Clos Poulet is also the place where wealthy burghers from Saint-Malo built their country houses. These families made great fortunes as seafaring merchants, privateers and arms dealers in the service of French kings. Many were ennobled and built elegant town houses for winter residence, country estates for summer – the famous *malouinières*, very different from Breton manor houses of earlier date. Chateaubriand admires their great ostentation, continuing, 'Sometimes the gardens descend to the sea framed by arches of lime trees, through a colonnade of pines, below a lawn; over the heads of the tulips of a parterre the sea presents its ships, its calm and its tempests.'

The Malouinière du Bos, listed by Chateaubriand among the most elegant, was built by the prestigious Magon family between 1715 and 1717. Of this family, people used to say: in Paris the Bourbons, in Saint-Malo the Magons. Such a proud race had a château bigger than most of the others, directly inspired by Parisian models in its architecture. Today the domain has preserved a fine unity of style, both in the buildings and the formal parterres to the north, their curve echoing that of the façade above. Their marble statues depicting the four seasons are Italian, brought back by traders who transported cod to Genoa and returned with their holds full of works of art. Sculptural detailing on the building appropriately depicts the heads of Mars, god of war, Aeolus, god of wind, and Mercury, god of commerce.

The name 'Bos' derives from a Viking word meaning refuge, echoing ancient invasions which have left traces at

nearby Saint Suliac. Variously spelt, it has always been pronounced 'bo'.

On the upper eastern edge of the domain, the chapel is a highlight for visitors thanks to its fine Louis XV *boiseries* and for pilgrims who still celebrate two festivals a year here. At the lower western edge lies the potager, which, still today, occupies no less than six thousand square metres. Nearby stand the outhouses and service buildings, constructed just after the château. An inventory made in 1840 lists a barnyard, press, laundry, storage cellar, caretakers' house, three stables, cowsheds, a chicken coop, and two pigsties.

War and commerce on the high seas are today distant echoes at the Malouinière. The Picard family has lived at the Malouinière du Bos since 1976. Their five children and eleven grandchildren frequently fill up the twenty rooms and go boating at Saint-Malo. Much of the potager's produce goes to feed the family, although, says Madame Picard, they are more interested in the eating than the picking. She indulges them except for green beans – there the rule is that everyone harvests his own.

The domain is peaceful, beauty and productivity now happily interwoven. Two fields each of a half-hectare flanking the formal parterre have been planted with large blocks of kiwis on arbours to the west, hazelnut bushes to the east. In a good year the family cannot consume the harvests of either, but since the plantations are essentially decorative, not every year is good. Before their installation, local farmers were always asking to use this land to graze a horse, or put in a potato crop. These permanent plantings ensure privacy and give pleasure. Elsewhere there are long strips of small fruit bushes, and a field of artichokes. In some years, the latter are invaded by aphids. Since the Picards refuse to use chemical pest controls, they simply let the artichokes flower. The palate regrets but the eye rejoices.

Fruit and vegetable gardening is done by a strong young

ABOVE : The beautiful eighteenth-century farm buildings and stables now house the caretakers at the Malouinière du Bos.

LEFT : Artichokes not eaten will be allowed to flower.

man from a local farming family who knows about plants and soil. The formal gardens are tended by a specialized landscaping firm which from the start undertook their restoration, based on the original eighteenth-century plans. But besides these professionals, the strongest earth spirit of the Malouinière du Bos is Jackie, a local character who is both gardener and mason, and who shares the Picards' considerable pride in the domain. Jackie lovingly restores and repairs some sixteen hundred metres of high walls which driving rains and windstorms regularly knock down. Most were originally built in 1717 with only earth to hold the stones together.

Madame Picard remains head gardener however. When picking a salad for supper, she may well get caught up in the weeding and stay much longer than she intended. Monsieur Picard may linger with his fourteen hives – beekeeping is a passion he has pursued since boyhood. The estate is rich with the plants which bees love, from the regal limes of the north lawn to the lavenders and santolinas which in part outline the formal parterre, to the locust trees (*Robinia pseudoacacia*) of the wood and the sage, lemon, wormwood, thyme and rosemary planted near the vegetables.

The star local vegetables are represented: peas, cauliflowers and potatoes. The Picards like the red potatoes for roasting and the white ones for purées, but grow several kinds from the earliest to the long winter keepers. Among the artichokes is the violet Prince of Brittany variety, but Madame Picard considers that this is really just the Provençal favourite, maturing two weeks later in Brittany. The microclimates by the Rance are not so far removed from those of southern France however: oleanders and mimosa survive outdoors here except in the coldest winters. A palm tree soars proudly into the Breton sky by the gate to the estate, near the stone tower which once served to house ice regularly brought by sailing ship from Norway.

Given this climate, the potager remains productive even in winter, when leeks, black radishes and winter lettuce can be left in the ground as well as different types of cauliflower. The Picards both grew up in families with vegetable gardens. They cultivate common varieties, and prepare their vegetables in the time-honoured manner of *cuisine bourgeoise*. Nothing is rare, everything is traditional – and of the best quality. What kind of pumpkins do they grow? The usual, says Madame Picard, the ones that grow big enough to serve as Cinderella's carriage.

Bretons, so they say, are born with sea water round their hearts. La Malouinière du Bos has the best of both worlds, with salt and spring water, sea and land, a life of comfort and elegance maintained with care.

ABOVE : Sixteen hundred metres of stone walls at La Malouinière du Bos...
RIGHT : The inlet of La Rance, behind the kiwi plantation.

Heirloom vegetables

More and more châteaux are sponsoring lively annual plant fairs involving heirloom fruit and vegetables, though that of Saint-Jean-de-Beauregard is still the most famous. Sometimes whole villages are the site of fairs, such as the squash and pumpkin extravaganza held at Tranzault in the Indre. Every year the number of events and associations increases as does, thankfully, the list offered by nurseries and seed merchants.

Yet gardeners today are still far from having the breadth of choice available before World War I. In 1867 the horticulturalist William Robinson, best known for his book *The Wild Garden*, visited Paris with a view to studying the city's produce markets which he judged far superior to Covent Garden both in the variety offered and the methods of culture and commercialization which made this possible. But although the French were triumphant with salads and radishes, asparagus and mushrooms, British beets remained superior in his opinion. He makes no judgment on cabbage.

Most striking today in Robinson's account is the tremendous range of vegetable varieties not only available but regularly consumed in 1867. 'The Parisians,' he noted, 'make much use of that delicate, wholesome and excellent vegetable Seakale'. He found not only artichokes (used in every Parisian restaurant) but cardoons, and many potato varieties, the earliest being the Marjolin grown on slopes above the Bois de Boulogne. 'Good King Henry' (*Chenopodium bonus-henricus*), similar to spinach and 'a really good and delicate vegetable' was commonplace in private gardens, as was 'Arroche or Orach', both red and white, and 'bulbous chervil', along with 'such leguminous plants as have curious snail-like seed vessels'. Called *chenillettes*, these were used to decorate salads as imitation snails...

Robinson's list of beans ('grown and used to a degree of which we can have but a poor conception' and 'used every day

in winter, in the smallest as well as in the grandest restaurants in Paris') is overwhelmingly sad to read today, when choice has shrunk so tremendously. And what should we think of his lament that the sweet potato, of which Louis XV was so excessively fond that he had it grown in the gardens of the Trianon and Choisy-le-Roi, had become so rare that only three varieties were commonly cultivated: the red, the yellow New Orleans, and the violet! Only in the 1990s has the most common orange sweet potato become readily available again in French supermarkets, and most customers view it as an American or Caribbean import hitherto unknown in French cuisine.

LEFT : Medieval harvesting of gourds and a drastic fifteenth-century form of pruning fruit trees.

*RIGHT : Green Climbing Melon (*Melon vert à rames, *Vilmorin).*

*FAR LEFT : Small Chinese Turban Gourd (*Giraumon petit de Chine, *Vilmorin).*

A voice in the wilderness:
François Harvey
in the Languedoc

Among the earliest pioneers and still in the avant-garde of the French seed saver movement is François Harvey, who has devoted his life to the propagation of rare vegetables. François and his wife Simone live in the wild Cévennes hills of central France, at the end of a long, bumpy and narrow dirt road which suddenly disappears leaving only mule tracks and a scattered hamlet of rustic stone houses. Theirs is the most isolated. From their door, a series of pocket gardens unfolds down the steep hillside, the lowest lying a whole kilometre from the house. Each one occupies a separate terrace backed by natural rock and stone walls one to three metres high, and each has a different size and shape. For

ABOVE : The fascinating Museum Garden of Limeuil in the Dordogne displays period potagers from prehistoric to modern times, with many varieties of physalis.

RIGHT : François Harvey grows dozens of different squashes and pumpkins, which need careful hand pollination to preserve the purity of each variety.

centuries no path connected them other than the rocky bed of a stream, dry in summer. But François, consolidating and rebuilding walls, has also made a footpath all the way to the broadest and most fertile stretches at the bottom of the valley. Around and among the spaces he cultivates are small bits of woodland and sloping meadows, jutting outcrops and huge boulders which sometimes shelter pools and reservoirs – some man-made, some natural.

These picturesque terrace potagers, which François describes as being 'enclosed in nature', shelter one of France's most extraordinary collection of heirloom and rare vegetables.

Blue potatoes, green, black or orange tomatoes, yard-long beans and lablabs, square-podded and asparagus peas, edible canna lilies and chrysanthemums, chayote (also called christophine or mirliton), a wide range of oriental greens and radishes, many hot and sweet peppers, different types of ground-nuts, Cape gooseberries and other physalis – the list of plants François produces is endless. Two plant families particularly attract him: the solanums, of which potatoes and tomatoes are the best known members, and the cucurbits, or pumpkins, marrows and courgettes. In the first group, for example, can be found an ancestor of modern tomatoes called *Lycopersicon hirsutum*, or a variety from Madagascar which keeps two to three months in storage, or many miniature tomatoes like those yellow ones which grow in clusters the size of grapes; or the elegant 'melon-pear' which is in fact a kind of aubergine. François has grown some ninety varieties of tomatoes and even more cucurbits, both edible and inedible, domestic and wild, all meticulously photographed in full and cross section and carefully labelled. His favourite tomatoes include the enormous one called Russian, the Fire Flag, the Téton de Venus, the black, the Green Zebra and, perhaps best of all, the tasty Valencia. He likes the American squashes Hubbard and Butternut but also the blue one of Hungary, and the Votavoa from Madagascar.

François grows vegetables on a total area of about two thousand square metres. A road circling round to the valley's end allows François to bring in cow manure by tractor to the bottom of the slope, but it must be distributed from there,

uphill, by wheelbarrow. Similarly the tractor brings harvests back up to the house. Inevitably on such a site, there is much surface composting.

Unusual in the Cévennes, this is a limestone valley where evergreen and white oaks, box, baytrees and terebinths typical of the Provençal *garrigue* thrive better than the sweet chestnut tree which long fed and still symbolizes the region generally. In its climate, this valley marks the very boundary of Mediterranean and mountain worlds: olive trees survive here

only in specially protected places. The serpentine terraces provide many microclimates which François uses to full advantage however.

Several smaller, upper terraces are devoted to one or two crops only: chick-peas, or a mixture of aromatic sage and zinnias to sell in the market, grown in a pretty spiral following the line of the hose which waters them. A collection of regional wild flowers and flowering shrubs surrounds stone benches on a small terrace entered by a little wooden gate. A botanical garden project was abandoned because the spot proved particularly attractive to wild boars. Only a large swath of tansy has survived.

The first big potager space hangs over the river bed, and is crammed with long lines of fennel, cardoons, beans, root crops, edible chrysanthemums and a brilliant stand of very decorative purple-leafed *Perilla frutescans*, appreciated in Vietnamese cuisine. Further down, another broad terrace shows off a mix of lavender, the first tomato varieties, licorice and rare radishes, edged with daylilies and yellow asphodel. Two long terraces by the river have been reserved for potatoes, and are sown with sky-blue flowering phacelia out of season.

The broad bottom terraces offer the widest range on five separate levels. A long arbour supports a kiwai vine (a hairless kiwi), squash vines and chayotes. Tree dahlias grow four metres high, ordinary dahlias are interplanted with curly-leaved parsley, yard-long beans, Chinese vegetables, and a number of medicinal plants.

Below spreads an entire field of tomatoes, surrounded by rambling pumpkins, hot and sweet peppers, and huge happy clumps of blue-flowered Mauritanian convolvulus. The lowest level of all is a sea of carefully labelled cucurbits, about fifty varieties in any given year. All are pollinated by hand, the flowers protected by little envelopes so that the seeds will reproduce faithfully for the next generation. Along the edge of this terrace grow annual daturas and small fruit bushes. Off to one side is a lovely rock cistern of clear water which always runs at 8–10° C.

All these crops are remarkably healthy. No one knows with certainty how old these terraces are. Since the ones just rebuilt look as if they had been there for ever, they might equally well date from the twelfth or eighteenth century. In 'the old days', they were planted with swedes, cabbage, chick-peas, broad beans and the Lozère variety of drought-resistant squash. But most were used for spring crops, put in and harvested before the heat of summer.

A tall, gangling, gentle man with a curly red beard and hair like a halo, François has become a well-known figure at the bi-weekly street market of the nearby village of Lasalle.

ABOVE : the Provençal bottle gourd or pilgrim's squash (Lagenaria cougourda*).*

LEFT : François Harvey's treasures on terraces in the heart of a wild valley in the Cévennes.

*ABOVE : This comic cucumber (*Cucumis metuliferus*) called kiwano, metulon or 'horny cucumber', is much appreciated in oriental cooking.*

RIGHT : Harvey specializes also in the Solanum family which includes many poisonous as well as many essential food plants, among which are tomatoes and potatoes.

Here he helped make popular vegetables now common but barely known in France twenty years ago when he began: black radishes for example, both the round and long varieties, or Chinese cabbage, or parsnips which appeal especially to his English customers. He has created a faithful local public for his edible cannas. Sometimes when he does not have enough of a crop to sell, he gives the vegetables away. One year this was Peruvian physalis, appropriately called goldenberries, its fruit growing in decorative tissue paper lantern pods. Today these appear on the table of every fashionable chef. François also sells seeds of rare vegetables on the market and by mail order to connoisseurs all over France. He has a solid reputation among collectors, without advertising or seeking to expand.

The Harveys lead a frugal and demanding life. Being tenants, they have never bothered to install running water in the house. Any spare cash from their modest commercial activity has been saved to allow François' vegetable seed collecting expeditions – to Madagascar and China and soon, he hopes, to Chile. Simone, her corn-paper hand-rolled cigarette hanging from the side of her mouth, Bogart style, has a quick wit more reminiscent of city cafés than the country kitchen where she turns huge buckets of hand-picked wild fruit (blueberries, dogwood berries, rose hips) into jams, preserves and vinegars for the market. In mid-November, François moves up and down the valley like a goat, wearing only leather sandals, fearing neither puddles nor torrents, nor the nettles which he picks to make infusions to treat plants and to sell, and as yet another vegetable for delicious soups.

Their landlords live on the hillside above them, in a working farm complete with goats, horses, a cow and a donkey. The Harveys also have some animals: chickens for eggs, dogs and cats, but nothing which needs to be slaughtered. François explains with a smile that he could not even manage to kill a rabbit. Vegetables are his obsession, and their lives revolve around this. But at the same time, the austerity of the site and their way of living is lightened by generosity and a sense of harmony. All of the vegetable plots are bright with flowers.

A knowledgeable garden historian, François points out the enormous losses of varities already incurred at the beginning of this century. Government agencies have so far, he feels, expended their efforts on limiting available varieties rather than increasing their number – at one point establishing an official, restrictive list. So much so that the Baumaux seed company was brought to court for including in its catalogue varieties not officially approved! Baumaux won the case and the list was discontinued.

The collection of rarities which François has assembled is not an attempt to re-create the past in any immediate or local sense, but rather an effort to maintain a kind of seed bank of vegetable varieties in danger of extinction. He is always looking for something new, and his personal Holy Grail would be the Baleine squash cited by Vilmorin in 1900 and undiscoverable by any collector in recent times.

Today François Harvey is not alone in his crusade to preserve the richest possible vegetable heritage. Another early pioneer was Victor Renaud, journalist and author of several books on the subject, who regularly attends the most important plant fairs to display the produce of his own experimental garden. In a contribution to a book published by an association of peasant writers (*Témoignages des écrivains paysans*), Renaud lamented the mechanization and industrialization of agriculture in the 1950s, and the F1 hybrids and *in vitro* multiplication which did not prove satisfying substitutes for the varieties lost. Such hybrids, he claimed, were developed for their carrying and storage qualities, not for flavour or adaptability to local conditions. He wondered about their famous pest and disease resistance, since the same companies which developed the hybrids also sold the chemical products for treatments... He later published a book on rare and forgotten vegetables and most recently one on 'natural' gardening, which bears witness to the success of his efforts to reach the public through these last decades.

The movement is growing, the public receptive, the range available for the table gradually increasing thanks to these gardeners like François Harvey, who, to quote once again Olivier de Serres, that great promoter of biodiversity, 'furnish as useful ornament of our household, innumerable species of roots, herbs, flowers and fruit, with many marvels'.

LE CHÂTEAU DES PÊCHEURS

The potager of the fairy-tale Château des Pêcheurs near Gien was restored by Edouard André in the 1920s. It still has iris, peonies and roses (White Pet and Honorine de Brabant for example) dating from that time. The graceful frame of an even older greenhouse, bereft of its glass, now supports grape vines, vigorous squash plants and rambling roses as a backdrop for the well-stocked herb garden.

Many heirloom vegetables can be found at the Château des Pêcheurs: red and white kohlrabi, soyabeans, orange pattipan and Siamese squashes, giant kale, all intermingled with daylilies, gaura, Mexican or giant hyssop and poppies set out in formal patterns. Perhaps the most savoury names are those of the old pear trees: Triomphe de Vienne, Bon Laboureur, Merveille Ribet, Beurré Clairgeau, and Frangipane among them. The owner, Madame de Chasseval, is ever concerned for the pleasure of her visitors, growing giant pumpkins for children to climb on. A lively plant fair is held here every April. But the potager is above all tended by and for a large and enthusiastic family.

II

GRASSROOTS GARDENING

ABOVE : French Breakfast Radish (Radis demi-long à bout blanc, *Vilmorin).*

PAGE 56 : Young courgettes in the garden of chef Robert Husser, of the Auberge du Cerf in Marlenheim (Alsace).

order): potatoes, green salads, tomatoes, and carrots, with a strong trend also towards green beans and leeks. An average of one quarter of the vegetables produced are given away to friends and neighbours.

Styles, however, have changed radically in the last fifty years. An article in the anniversary issue of *Le Jardin du cheminot*, the railway employees' gardening magazine, summarized the evolution of the family garden in France starting with the victory gardens of World War II, when all the parks of Paris produced vegetables and France numbered some 700,000 allotments. After the post-war housing crisis, an urban boom played down country roots in the euphoria of modern appliances and paid holidays. Subsequently, especially after 1968, there was a nostalgic return to the earth and a war between organic methods and chemicals in gardening as in agriculture. And finally, by 1993, more and more families were observed living outside major cities, blending urban and country ways in a more ecologically balanced mode.

Today, every country road, every tiny hamlet in deepest France reveals small kitchen gardens, tucked into the most unlikely corners at times – half under a bridge, or on steep slopes. Everywhere they add changing colour and texture to the tapestry of France's rural landscapes.

Country gardens

Country potagers, those belonging to farmers and peasants, traditionally had clearly defined customs. First of all, they were generally worked by women. The presence of flowers is often attributed to this feminine care. Jean Taillemagre in his personal memoirs of *La Vie aux champs* records that the peasants he knows shrug their shoulders when asked about *le jardin*, saying 'that's women's work'. Taillemagre however judges that 'flowers refine the country woman. In looking after them, she learns about harmonies of colour and gesture'. He recalls a peasant household where the mother and daughters made such elegant bouquets for table and sideboard that their men, even after a hard day in the fields, began to wash and change for dinner. This author adds that you can

Gardening in France has become a national passion. The statistics are truly impressive: according to an official government survey published in 1994, half of French households possess some sort of garden, two-thirds of which include vegetables or fruit. Nor are all these plots found in rural areas: twenty per cent of city dwellers spend time gardening. The average French gardener is about thirty-five years of age, may equally well be man or woman, has two children and spends (in the mid 1990s) an average of 1400 francs (approx £150) a year on the garden. His or her favourite vegetables are (in descending tell the prosperity of a farmstead from the quality of its kitchen garden.

Peasant gardens in the 1990s are still worked largely by women. Their men still take on the heavier labours of the fields and do, at times, begrudge water for flowers among the vegetables. They sometimes change their minds at retirement, however, when they may start to garden themselves. If retired parents live with working children, the older people grow the vegetables – and flowers – for the entire family.

In other groups, the division of labour may be different, though still by sex. The railway workers' gardening magazine began to publish a special column on flowers in the 1950s – intended for wives. First devoted to dahlias (the cactus varieties were popular) and chrysanthemums (pompons and cas-

cades) it soon announced the arrival of new roses, especially the successful Madame Meilland, and later the introduction from America by the Vilmorin-Andrieux company of Giant Pacific delphiniums. The men were expected to continue with vegetables though in practice there were many exceptions.

Today, the term 'peasant' like 'worker' is harder to define and formerly distinct categories slide together. Most rural vegetable gardeners now have, or have had, some other professional activity besides farming. One thing is clear: at a time when the garden press thrives as never before, few country gardens, however remotely rural, are entirely unselfconscious. Everyone today cares how their garden looks, not only how much it produces. 'The garden, that interior dream made manifest,' writes poet Marie Rouanet, 'first of all for the eye'.

Country kitchen gardens are still often the domain of women gardeners, but the whole family may turn out to help harvest.

Cliff dwellers at Labeaume in the Ardèche

Many country gardens today are cultivated by the children of peasants who have been to town and back again. In poor regions like the south-centre part of France, many rural towns now largely emptied of their agricultural populations survive mainly as centres for summer tourism. Farmers' children were already migrating from here to urban centres decades ago, aspiring to the economic security of government jobs with the railway or the postal service. Many returned to the country after retirement. But today more and more attempt to find work *au pays* when still young. Thus Monsieur and Madame F..., after living some years in Paris, moved home to an inherited farmhouse near Labeaume in 1982.

Monsieur F...'s job as a postman leaves him time to garden, a passion he pursues with an unusual curiosity about local traditions as well as techniques. His wife stays at home since the birth of their three youngsters, but finds time to help sow some seven kilos of bean seed and preserve over eighty litres of green beans in a season. The potager clearly lies at the heart of this family's existence.

This cliff-hugging Ardèche potager contains as much rock as earth. Stone reverberates heat, which can help ripening.

The Vivarais province, situated in the south of the Ardèche, made headlines in 1994 when local speleologists discovered the Chauvet grottoes near Vallon-Pont d'Arc. The whole region contains limestone labyrinths and deep river beds where vestiges of prehistory can be turned up every day with a spade. Monsieur F... has thus uncovered many arrow-heads, pottery shards, and a primitive scraping tool. In this department where local cuisine has for centuries been based on the sweet chestnut, scientists have estimated the age of one mummified chestnut as no less than 8.5 million years! The very name of the town Labeaume means 'grotto'. The River Baume runs by the foot of the village, its pebble beaches full of swimmers in summer, who admire the towering peak of the Rocher de Sampson in the distance topped now by a television mast. But Monsieur F... specifies that the caves and grottoes of his native commune, though created like those of nearby Chauvet from the action of water on huge blocks of limestone, remain small-scale in comparison.

It is a subject he knows well, for his house sits right at the edge of a sheer, luminous, limestone bluff full of crevices carved by the temporary torrents of spring and autumn rain. All up and down the cliff face, earlier generations created a maze of small, walled terraces to shore up shallow topsoil for cultivation. The result is a picturesque tapestry of vegetable plots linked together among wilder slopes here by small flights of steps, there by narrow and precarious paths. Until World War II, this land was cultivated for spring vegetables only. The reverberating heat of the white chalk favoured early crops, but made summer production well nigh impossible – though old-timers knew especially adapted varieties of lettuce that were slow to bolt, or drought-resistant aubergine.

Only at the foot of the hill were there broader spaces available for more traditional plantings. The ruins of an old mill across the river suggest that its banks were once sown with wheat.

Labeaume boasted over one thousand inhabitants in 1900, but now the town supports less than half this population. One hundred years ago there were as many as sixteen olive mills in this commune alone, now there are none. The remaining peasant families prefer to cultivate more fertile, easy-to-irrigate plots near the river. It takes the courage and curiosity of energetic young people like the F...s to persist on such difficult – but such beautiful – terrain. And indeed, for these farmers' children who have been to Paris and returned, beauty is part of the appeal.

Their eighteenth-century family farmstead is now enclosed on three sides by a kind of rural suburbia, near a large holiday village. On the side seen from the road, their restoration pays homage to the modern aesthetic of such communities with terracotta pigeons around a painted dovecote, and wrought iron decorations. In this part of the garden, they have experimented with exotic trees such as spruce and Austrian pine. But on the open cliff front, where the house looks out over river valley, they have preserved and enhanced the local character of the site. The south-eastern façade of the house is now shaded in summer by a broad trellis arbour on which different table grapes prosper – a local variety called Isabelle produces

ABOVE : Stone walls can provide tool storage, or water resevoirs, or simply hold back earth.

LEFT : Each tiny pocket of earth grows something: six cabbages surround a young olive tree.

big, juicy fruit by mid-August. There is also a wisteria which, like the vines, comes late into leaf to let sunshine heat the house in winter, and provide shade – and flower and scent – in late spring and summer.

From here the garden unfolds its patterns of rough out-croppings, often coloured by patches of yellow or orange stonecrop and lichens and bands of iris jutting out between wider strips of vegetables. Everything is on a small scale – modest differences in level, stone walls only metres long. Many of these upper terraces have nonetheless sacrificed space for low-clipped, squared off rosemary hedges along their outer edges. The resulting effect makes the concession worthwhile however, for the dense rosemary adds a fine dark line running parallel to both the brighter, luxuriant foliage of the vegetables and the pale retaining walls. In winter, it is lightened by the herb's brilliant blue flowers.

Here and there are rural objects – a rusty cartwheel, or a mysteriously carved stone, things found in the house itself during its restoration. There are round, square and long trian-gular spaces, some of which have also been planted with young olive trees. At their feet, grouped cabbages, chard and even car-doons enhance the mosaic effect. Other tiny terraces remain green – or grey – all through the year thanks to beds of lemon balm, thyme and sage. The untamed intervals of the lower slopes are invaded by young hackberries (*Celtis australis*), ever-green and white oaks, hogweed, and a prickly, sticky vine which has fragrant white flowers in September.

The site as a whole takes careful managing to retain still-existing topsoil and prevent further erosion. It is at times impossible to tell which bits of the precipice are natural and which are man-made. Monsieur F... has learned the essential art of water management on such a site, where a small but sturdy wall can block a crevice to provide a reservoir even on the steepest part of the cliff. This may provide just enough water to make up a batch of 'Bordeaux mixture' copper spray for the potatoes by the shore without having to climb back up to the house. The F...'s main source of water, however, is the river below. They pump up a generous supply even in summer, using sprinklers on timers for most vegetable plots. Indeed, it is this modern technology that is largely responsible for their

being able to garden on this site, abandoned by their elders.

Cisterns in the rockface also provide drinking water for their four sheep – merinos from Arles, plus a smaller black ram. Allowed to climb up and down the hillside, they keep grass down on paths and in wilder sections. But their presence means protecting cultivated terraces and young trees with wire fencing. Because he finds this ugly, Monsieur F... wonders about enclosing the sheep by the riverbank. Only then the mowing problem will remain.

Other animals live here – a dog, chickens, and beautiful pigeons which no longer fly free since a weasel killed twenty of them in a single night. On the whole however, domestic and wildlife co-exist peacefully, and the rare Bonelli's eagle can often be seen soaring against the southern sky.

Snails made a sudden onslaught on the bean crop in 1994, but generally vegetables are healthy here, greenfly unknown even on the roses growing by the house. No doubt exposure to wind and light as well as the garden's isolation discourage such pests. Certainly the growing conditions are special – some varieties of aubergine thrive (usually the long ones), others, even of those bought in the local markets, give up straight away. The F...s like to experiment with old varieties and buy many seeds from the connoisseur supplier, Baumaux. They prefer catalogues with ample illustrations. Monsieur F... likes to start everything from seed himself as much as possible, and has a small greenhouse in a separate plot behind the house where the cucurbits, strawberries and tomatoes grow.

When not picking and preserving vegetables and raising children, Madame F... likes to draw and paint. It is surely her aesthetic intuition as well as her husband's research into the past which has created this astonishingly patterned family potager on the cliff wall of Labeaume. Author Jean Giono's words about another site fit this one perfectly: 'A few old walls made golden with lichens hold up terraces decorated with geo-metric motifs of artichokes, the woolly pompons of broad beans or the blond floss of chick-peas and lentils; but from the balcony overlooking them, these colours lost their veg-etable values to achieve purely pictorial qualities, and it is thanks to the gardener's hoe that we penetrate the purely aesthetic pleasures of a painting'.

A village 'green zone' at Cajarc in the Lot

Halfway between the rural family's home garden and the big city allotments are the green zones growing around even small towns. Unlike individual plots, they are separate from the gardener's residence although sometimes only by a few hundred metres; and unlike the urban patches rented for weekend cultivation, they generally belong to the people who work them.

These country green zones have also caught the eye of poets and painters, among them British novelist Ford Madox Ford, who discovered in the 1930s in Provence, '...a little territory of an extreme fertility where the Tarasconnais gardens in the evenings and erects the little huts that serve for weekend cottages... The moment the shades of evening begin to fall he is up and away from desk or counter and wading amongst the profusions of his melon-patch, his pumpkins, his gourdes, pimenti and his tomatoes'.

The smallest market communities in the most isolated provinces still display such strips and stripes, usually sited along the river or stream on which the town was built. Such gardens provide a kind of missing link between country and city kitchen gardens, largely unrecognized by garden historians much taken today with urban allotments. But they are everywhere present in rural France.

In the Quercy region of south-western France, the Cahors road along the River Lot winds at times under overhanging cliffs, at others through clustered villages or past broad stretches of bank given over to market gardening – maize, asparagus, lettuce are common crops. The water becomes a broad, smooth

Narrow dirt paths wind through a multi-coloured maze by the river at Cajarc, in Quercy.

ribbon as it passes by the little town of Cajarc. Right behind the *bourg* rise the steep limestone-layered cliffs of the Causses.

At first glance, Cajarc seems sunk in remote, rural existence. Its population of a thousand doubles every summer however thanks to holidaymakers who enjoy its riverside scenery and quaint architecture, where bricks, stone, wood, tile and slate may all appear in the same house. Its great claim to celebrity in recent years has been engendering novelist Françoise Sagan.

But the town has long had deeper cosmopolitan connections. For centuries, the peaceful stream which today gives pleasure mainly to tourists and boaters carried down to Bordeaux a surprising variety of locally produced commodities. Tobacco was grown in Cajarc from 1824. Wines from Cajarc once went to market as 'Bordeaux' but the vines were killed by the dreaded phylloxera a hundred years ago. Lumber and coal came through from upstream and were also carried down to Bordeaux, and boats brought back spices from the East, and dried cod from America.

Land along the river in an area named La Ségalière (because of the rye – *seigle* – grown there for straw, used for caning chairs) was sold at auction by the town council in the mid-nineteenth century, in the form of fifteen vegetable garden lots, averaging twenty metres wide. Buyers included a justice of the peace, two masons, an innkeeper, a blacksmith, two shoemakers, a woodworker, a police commissioner and a lemonade seller. This choice alluvial land soon fell into the possession of the well-to-do, however, and was cultivated by hired hands. One elderly owner today remembers purchasing his strip from a banker who still had liveried servants. The poorer villagers managed stony plots on the cliffs behind, where rare rainwater was collected in cisterns much as at the F...s, and good valley earth sometimes brought up by oxcart.

The old railway line still runs on a ridge parallel to the river, but is used now only for a little tourist train. On the strip of land between railway and river the patchwork of potagers still exists. Access to the plots at La Ségalière is provided by the former towpath, ending in a medieval sailors' chapel, and also by a more recent public walk on newly

ABOVE : Lime flowers make good herbal tea, with incomparable flavour when freshly picked.

LEFT : The riverfront strip has been reclaimed for a public path.

ABOVE : Asked about fruit preserves, gardeners in this region think more readily of eau de vie *than of jam...*

RIGHT : No fast-assembled toolsheds here, but the same brick, stone and slate mixtures which characterize the local rural architecture.

reinforced banks under canopies of wild alders which the town trims and thins.

Once the promenade round the potagers was a favourite public stroll on Sundays. Today many townspeople prefer modern homes with their own garden away from the medieval centre. But if these gardens are no longer cultivated for proud display, some indeed showing sad neglect, the faithful still love to meet in the mornings, when mists rise from the river, and again at twilight. Low wire fences protect the plots from rabbits along the paths, bamboo stands hide some patches from the river walk, and various kinds of hedging separate one plot from the neighbour's. But there is never complete enclosure, and gardening here is a community activity still.

Monsieur Casseyre, whose family has lived in Cajarc since 1291, jokes that the town's major export today is civil servants, its major import retirees. Many of the older gardeners complain jovially that young people would rather play *boules* than work hard in a garden. But they will point out, just as cheerfully, that two owners now too old to work here themselves have between them a daughter and a nephew who come regularly. A small community of hard-working Portuguese also provides gardeners who pay rent in kind. The plot of the *curé* is kept clean by the good souls of the parish, but not cultivated. A dentist is suspected of buying a riverfront plot largely to moor his boat. And yet one of the most ambitious gardens belongs to a young man who works at the local post office and uses his wire fence to support sumptuous pumpkins that climb up into the branches of an old apple tree.

Monsieur Casseyre, once a civil servant himself and now retired, transformed his potager twenty years ago into a commercial orchard. At that time, the old varieties were still largely unavailable and so he grows such apples as Starking, Golden Delicious, Reine des Reinettes and Belle de Boskoop, with average yields of forty kilos per tree every year. All the trees have been cut into a kind of fruiting hedge, following the 'Bouché-Thomas' method developed in the Loire valley, which consists of bending the trunks at an angle of 35° with no particular pruning. The result is a complex network which

ABOVE : Dahlias count among the most beloved country garden flowers, often growing among the vegetables.

RIGHT : Villagers and visitors appreciate the peaceful industry of these plots, especially very early or late on a hot summer day.

would be beautiful were it not for the chicken-wire protection round each tree against the rabbits.

Madame Roque, wife of a retired local contractor, comes daily and indeed cannot stay away. Her potager intermingles fruit, vegetables, herbs and flowers in the best old tradition of plentiful exuberance. One pear tree (variety unknown) produces fruit weighing over half a kilo each – at first glance she mistook its windfalls for pumpkins that the children picked too soon. This same corner is filled with purple asters, which she knows as *vendangeuses* ('harvest flowers'). Elsewhere, sprinkled throughout, are clumps of evening primrose (which she calls *belles de nuit*), Chinese lanterns (*Physalis alkekengii*), hollyhocks, pansies, and rudbeckia, which she is careful to point out are NOT Jerusalem artichokes. A huge stand of purple-leafed amaranth was knocked over by wind.

Madame Roque's plot is formally divided in two by a central lane, crowded on both sides with flowering shrubs and small fruit bushes. Smaller, more winding paths are edged with chives, or the rather more invasive lambs' ears (*Stachys lanata*) and snow-in-summer (*Cerastium tomentosum*). There are many surprises, as she encourages self-sowing of chervil, parsley, gaillardia... Vegetables thrive right at the foot of a big tamarisk, or an apple tree with its branches propped up on stakes. A yucca has grown tall by the shed.

The soil is good, the site very protected. Madame Roque makes piles of compost here and there, though sometimes burning debris. A few years ago she remembers bringing in some manure. There is no set method, but obviously everything prospers. Even the bindweed turns out to be bellweed with huge white trumpets that are actually quite decorative. She grows 'Russian' tomatoes that weigh half a kilo each and which, she says, you eat raw like an apple. These she sows herself in little pots, but mostly buys her summer season vegetables already started, either at the Saturday afternoon market in town, or a bi-monthly fair. A keen cook, she is proud of making cassoulet with her own white beans already by the first Sunday in August, when Cajarc has its annual festival. Asked about fruit preserves, she first thinks of brandies rather than jams. Some locals still have the right to distill the white *eaux de vie* traditional in the region.

The main pests complained of by all the owners of these riverside plots are rabbits. Because of the railway line and its occasional tourist train in summer, shooting is forbidden in this part of town. Locals complain that rabbits may be seen sunning themselves on the tracks, openly taunting hunters. No one in these gardens has any domestic animal but hunting dogs – except for one man down the road who apparently raises ... rabbits.

Hunting and gathering in country towns remain the natural counterparts of growing food, especially in the south.

However Cajarc's green zone gardeners, even the retired civil servants, will never resemble Marcel Pagnol's Provençal poacher, who did not even have a potager, and could not tell a turnip from an artichoke: 'He bought all his vegetables and ate meat every day,' commented his farmer neighbour, 'just like a summer visitor'.

In France, as elsewhere, both city folk and farmers look askance at each other's oddities. But not all city dwellers today can afford to eat meat on a daily basis, much less to take holidays in the sun. For many such in recent years, the annual summer exodus to the south has been replaced with – vegetable gardening!

Community gardens

City kitchen gardens today may occupy plots in the back garden or, in a growing number of cases, land provided by a municipality. Town councils make an effort to keep these areas accessible both geographically and financially, and find indeed that in most places it is hard to keep up with a growing and insistent demand. There are already some 4600 at Strasbourg, 3500 at Lyons, 1200 at Tours.

Allotments or community gardens, as they are sometimes called, have a special history in France and owe their existence largely to the vision of one man: the Abbé Lemire, deputy for the department of the Nord, who in 1896 founded the Ligue Française du Coin de Terre et du Foyer (French League for Earth and Hearth). This far-seeing reformer also worked to establish an active ministry for labour, the six-day week, health and retirement benefit, and family allowances. As early as 1876 he participated in the founding of the still active Societé d'Horticulture by a group of miners at Valenciennes. French Academy author Marguerite Yourcenar remembers meeting the Abbé Lemire in 1918, when she was a small child: 'This was clearly someone who never worried about the effect he produced on others.' She considers the Abbé to be one of only three men encountered in her long existence who possessed 'a faultless integrity'.

Allotments began when the Abbé persuaded factory owners and charitable patrons to donate land for working-class gardens, intended to be the humble equivalent of the industrialists' weekend villa. With one important difference right from the start: these plots never belong, now as then, to those who work them but are rented, either from a managing association or directly from a municipality. This ensures that anyone not keeping his plot shipshape may be expelled. It also means however that the gardener risks forfeiting his land if the city expropriates it, or, in the case of job-related rentals, if he is fired. Precarious tenancy of land continues to be a major problem.

The first *jardins ouvriers* or working mens' gardens were intended exclusively for men, designed to provide breathing space for husbands and fathers caught between factories and equally airless hovels at home. Women and children were allowed only at weekends. Nonetheless, the preservation of the family was the Abbé's prime goal: 'If the earth provides the means, the family must remain the end.' Kitchen gardens kept the men out of *cabarets* (the nineteenth-century French equivalent of the English pub) and helped them to provide healthy produce for home consumption (but not for resale). The term 'heads of family' appears in the original statutes, and today the inclusion of single women with children has proven problematic on some sites.

In recent years, the term *jardins ouvriers* has been quite deliberately replaced by *jardins familiaux* or 'family gardens' to correspond to a changing membership. Industrial collectives – those linked to a particular activity or enterprise such as the railway – still thrive, especially in the north. But the Ligue, now often called the Fédération Nationale des Jardins Familiaux, has adjusted its aims, like its name, to contemporary conditions. Its allotment gardens were once intended to help people alienated by their working conditions, explains spokesman Philippe Pierson, whereas today they often alleviate the alienation of those who have no work at all.

Similarly, if the original plot consoled country people obliged to migrate to the city to find work, today many offer solace to immigrant workers from outside France. In Schiltigheim near Strasbourg, some seventeen different nationalities are represented. In the industrial community of Roubaix, forty-five per cent of allotment gardeners are immigrants. There are now also allotments for the handicapped – in Morangis (Essonne), or at the Institut des Terres-Noires, at La Roche-sur-Yon (Vendée), where some four hectares of gardens were developed in the late 1980s as workhops to stimulate 120 mentally handicapped children.

Thus a major goal has become the rehabilitation of people in difficulty of any kind. The Fédération's 1993 charter, co-signed by the Minister of the Environment, states clearly that its potagers are available to people of all origins and social

ABOVE: City allotment gardens in France were originally the pride and joy of the men of the house, a week-end refuge from industrial jobs.

LEFT: Early Nantes Carrot (Carotte rouge demi-longue nantaise, Vilmorin).

backgrounds, intended to provide both leisure activity and an economic resource for the underprivileged.

Today's Fédération and the allotment movement generally take a firm stand against the two negative connotations from which they have sometimes suffered: nineteenth-century industrial paternalism and the Pétain connection during World War II. Inevitably, the war period marked a great boom in urban vegetable gardening all over the country: in 1946 there were 700,000 allotment gardens. Today, when the numbers are closer to 150–200,000, the Fédération insists on self-government through gardeners' asociations, of which there are some eight hundred.

Municipal aid is a must. But this is no longer in any sense philanthropic, for the Fédération's gardens offer many advantages to the townships which help support them. Allotment gardens can be situated on land otherwise left fallow and unfit for construction – along rivers, for example, where flooding may occur. Vegetable gardening, it is claimed, may even help reduce river pollution. The average cost of laying out and equipping such plots is only one fifth that of any ordinary city park for the same area. And these kitchen garden belts can be integrated into public spaces, with playgrounds, nature and jogging trails, and more conventional parkland around them. They help vary the texture of urban décors. About a fifth of the allotments existing today are estimated to include such public areas, in Colmar, for example, or at Tulle in the Limousin. Schoolchildren are more and more present, either simply for outings where they often see living vegetables for the first time, or to gain actual experience, when they grow a little plot of produce themselves.

Allotment associations have varying arrangements with the cities that provide their land, concerning a collective

Ragmens' gardens at Saint-Ouen, c. 1900.

water supply, path and road networks, rubbish disposal, insurance and the building of sheds or shelters. The financing of these gardens thus varies a good deal. Only about half the allotment associations in France belong to the Fédération. Its spokesman, Monsieur Pierson, looks longingly to Germany where all such clubs belong to a single organism, and any outsiders lose their subsidies. The French remain, as they love to say with pride, more 'individualistic'. The main bone of contention is aesthetic, particularly as concerns the look of built elements, restricted by the Abbé Lemire's original statutes to a tool shed (*cabane*) and an arbour (*tonnelle*).

While in northern Europe and Germany, allotment gardeners construct real cottages and weekend homes on their land, this is forbidden in France both by rule and by the very precariousness of the land's tenancy, which encourages makeshift installations. Originally, everyone made his own shed, however ramshackle, using bits of recycled materials according to need and whim. The Fédération needs to enlist municipal support for its associations and cannot afford to encourage shantytown gardening, which town councils see as eyesores rather than assets. Today it has spent much time and effort exploring techniques to produce cheap kits to make efficient sheds and shelters – inevitably the same throughout any one green zone, though quite variable from town to town. Critics therefore accuse the Fédération of suppressing popular creativity and imposing uniformity.

Allotment gardens are certainly organized on a collective model, and this means constraints on individual initiatives. Adherents are expected to work hard, both in the garden and in association activities. No one may exploit land for commercial aims (a rule which has sometimes been bent in small ways, if only to cover costs). Animals are generally forbidden, but today many keep a few rabbits or chickens. Certainly a good number of urban gardeners today share the Abbé's desire for a well-policed arrangement of respectable appearance. There are many competitions to present the best-looking plot.

Sociologist Florence Weber makes some interesting generalizations about city allotment gardeners. Working-class participants do not take pride, she says, in the flavour and quality of their produce, an aim reserved for bourgeois gourmets. Nor in the abundance of their crops, as peasants or those who have recently left the country may do. Rather their goal is perfect order, a beautifully aligned grid without weeds, in a territory completely subjected to the personal control of the gardener, and indicative of his self-esteem. The Fédération's concern for order would therefore reflect the legitimate concerns of its members.

And if the community spirit imposes constraints, it also gives ample satisfactions. Allotment neighbourliness can count a lot for the chronically unemployed, the recently widowed, or anyone in distress overwhelmed by city indifference.

The Ivry citadel in Paris

Paris remains a special case, for nowhere else did the late nineteenth-century rural exodus produce such floods of immigrants, such a fast and vast expansion of the working classes as in the capital city. The *jardins ouvriers* here grew up to combat the particularly strong seduction of city *cabarets* (described by Zola in his novel *L'Assommoir*). Most were planted on the line where the city walls once stood. Today, this encircling green zone has been largely replaced by the fast ring road, the *boulevard périphérique*. Here and there as traffic roars inexorably round the city, drivers can still glimpse strips of vegetable gardens on higher slopes. But the most famous of all, the gardens of the Fort d'Ivry, lie well away from the flux. Being private property, open only on special public days, they continue to provide the haven of peace originally intended, although the high-rises of modern Paris stand out on the skyline behind the tomato plants of some of the higher plots.

The potagers of Ivry are remarkable in several respects: first in their site around a still operative army citadel, both in the broad moat, the *fossé*, and on the sloping rampart opposite, called the *glacis*. The walk round covers about three kilometres and includes some 248 irregularly numbered gardens. These average 250 square metres in size but come in all different shapes. Second, the association which manages these gardens allows a great deal of personal initiative in their design. As a result, the layouts and constructions of Ivry offer endless variety. And finally, because they form an unusually picturesque ensemble, the Fort d'Ivry gardens have had special appeal for television producers, photographers, journalists

The Ivry allotment management imposes no uniformity on its tenants over their garden shelters and fencing. Hence much colourful experimentation.

and writers such as Jean-Bernard Pouy, who set here his thriller *Belle de Fontenay*. Robert Doisneau took a famous long view of the moat gardens from the gate of number 225 high above.

Like all the *jardins ouvriers*, those of Ivry were born of a benevolent paternalism. In 1907, the Abbé Lemire met and inspired two Christian Socialists, Monsieur and Madame Marque, who then went on to create these gardens. Each Christmas, a great party was held at which Madame Marque particularly spoiled the children. Her husband, a pharmacist, remained president of the Association from 1908 to 1944 when both he and his wife were killed in Allied bombardments. At that time, there were over 200,000 allotment gardens in and around Paris alone.

In the 1960s, however, property values soared and much land was sold. Reduced to two thousand by 1970, the number of Parisian gardens climbed back up to 2800 by 1980. The hillside amphitheatre at Ivry, where once the great fêtes were held was itself cut up into garden plots which today count among the best situated and most beautiful of all. After a period of cultivation largely by retired couples, today's gardens are again a godsend for large families of modest means. But now many professional people also apply.

Since 1993, Dr Perreau has been president of the Ivry Association. He takes his office very seriously. For although Ivry offers its adherents more freedom than many, accepting gates of either metal or wood in different colours and even the classic, recycled, painted iron bedsteads, these gardens also must be well kept or their tenants are asked to leave. Retired people, for example, who disappear for three or four months a year to stay with children in some remote province, may risk losing their land. There is after all a long waiting list. Only ten to fifteen plots become available each year, and it may well take three years to get one. Therefore Dr Perreau and the four elected delegates regularly inspect all the gardens. The problem is not only unused space. Such absences endanger the social fabric so important in all of these gardens – the friendly competition, the exchange of cuttings and seeds. One spot at Ivry has even been set aside for *boules*.

ABOVE: Creativity is the keynote at Ivry: when the pumpkin grows, an old plank will be found to support it.

LEFT: Two levels at Ivry, the citadel wall and the moat, create a great variety of sheltered spaces.

ABOVE AND RIGHT : Regulations forbid overnight stays, but daytime use is rich and varied.

Although the camaraderie, here as elsewhere, has been traditionally masculine, more and more single women are gardening at Ivry. The good Dr Perreau wonders if they will prove as tidy as the men, and observes that those already installed seem better at decoration than at cultivation... One, however, a former nurse's aid, has become a noted specialist in aromatic and medicinal plants, and can often be met bicycling down the narrow paths with laden baskets.

The Association has regular meetings in the only shed which has electricity and heat. Outside, a spreading trellis arbour supports two kinds of succulent table grapes. In October it may also shelter a vast table full of piled up pumpkins, including the rarely found Citronnelle de Bergerac. Provincial vegetable varieties are as common here as regional accents. Allotment gardeners may originate from all over France and beyond, introducing new seeds and methods. But they also help preserve local ones: a turnip called Virtue of Aubervilliers is no longer found in catalogues but survives in the allotment gardens at ... Aubervilliers.

Almost all the plots produce flowers and fruit as well as vegetables. Cherry trees bloom in pale bouquets everywhere at Ivry in April. One gardener proudly proffers large, juicy figs in October. Here and there a sheltered, evergreen strawberry tree (*Arbutus unedo*) may manage to ripen its red berries even as it flowers in February. A good population of songbirds both protects and threatens fruit production, the blackbirds having a special fondness for grapes. Among the other perils of paradise in Ivry are underground tunnels remaining from earlier fortifications (the twenty forts of old Paris were once interconnected with underground passages). And there is the occasional theft from one plot to the next – gates are kept locked, on the whole.

But such separations as gates, hedging and bean-pole walls do not lessen the amiable conviviality of the place. Domestic animals are not, in theory, allowed, but a barky black Pomeranian, engaging in mock battles, has become the mascot of an entire section. Indeed Abbé Lemire's goal of family solidarity is fully realized when, as here, a father and son cultivate adjacent patches. His enemy, the *cabaret*, takes its revenge however during the neighbourly aperitif.

Above all, these allotments, at Ivry as elsewhere, become a great source of pride. The hard work of gardening is not like

doing a job for an employer. Efforts here reap the rewards of personal achievement. The gardener who has the first ripe tomatoes earns the admiration and envy of neighbours, in allotments as elsewhere. But here everyone gathers round, and wants to know how it was done. Each gardener knows every square centimetre of his or her own plot, but also keeps track of the neighbours' experiments: one plants rows running north-south one year, and east-west the next, another has just installed drip irrigation. Many brag as much about their friends as about themselves: 'You should go down to the one at the end, he's a real artist!'

The pride of these gardeners in their own creativity allows free rein to the humour which characterizes so many *jardins ouvriers*. Landscape architect Bernard Lassus visited some thousand such community gardens in the 1970s and describes their spirit of exuberant self-parody. The bedstead gate or the fancy wallpaper and plaster columns in a ramshackle shed may not be just examples of economical recycling, he claims, but also quite deliberate jokes. Imitation wells may be aggressively false reminders of a rural logic lost in the landscape of the passing motorway. Mockery of the limits imposed, of one's own desires, of middle-class solemnity – visual wit often echoes the teasing banter which helps neighbours put up with each other's foibles. And at times joviality may take on age-old pagan forms, such as the parade to honour St Fiacre where the men dress up as vegetables and ask the ladies to admire their carrots...

For Lassus, these gardens not only satisfy physical but also imaginative needs. Their décors may evoke other places, other spaces for living. A life-size statue of Snow White with a fawn sits on a well in a miner's garden in northern France, not looking at the vegetables nor even at the neighbours, but at the railway line and two slagheaps. Her presence and attitude, says Lassus, transform the industrial landscape she seems to admire into a powerful, though purely imaginary, forest.

Humour and dream lead to good humour – an essential ingredient in any paradise, but especially in these picturesque Edens where individual resourcefulness and creative *bricolage* are set in a collective context.

ABOVE : Garden shelters at Ivry are far more than tool sheds or places to dry garlic. They embody all the cheerful convivialilty and neighbourly spirit of the place.

LEFT : Pets are not encouraged, but cats and small dogs find their way here nonetheless.

The Ivry allotments may seem like Eden, but require hard work to maintain.

Today many gardeners on the Ivry waiting list, like those in other major urban centres, are often doctors and dentists. Things are different in more remote communities like the city of Tulle, a town of some sixteen thousand inhabitants in the Limousin. In spite of a particularly active community organization, many factory employees prefer to meet at rugby matches or card tournaments or the popular tea-dances. It is true that city allotments still thrive mostly in the predominantly industrial areas of France: the north, the Pays de Loire and the Rhône valley.

Amiens' floating islands

I f the Abbé Lemire forbade the selling of produce, this was in part to protect thriving urban populations of market gardeners (*maraîchers*). These have traditionally practised the famous art of French intensive gardening, too limited for agriculture but too professional to count as household activity. English horticulturalist William Robinson greatly admired the tight-knit community of market gardeners he met in Paris in the 1860s, visiting them at home on the edge of the city: 'Certainly in no part of Britain is the ground, whether garden or farm, as thoroughly cultivated or rendered nearly as productive as in these little family gardens as they may be called, for they are usually no longer than admits of the owners' eye telling the condition of every crop in the garden all at once.' He went on to note that these gardeners kept to themselves, intermarried, and seemed content to own only as much ground 'as gives occupation to their family'. This was generally no more than a hectare, walled in, furnished with a cottage and a well.

Robinson was invited for a glass of wine by one household of market gardeners, and two sunburnt, barefoot hired hands joined in unceremoniously, obviously considered to be 'part of the family'. Many of the owners, he says, were illiterate but kept a barometer, and had a mutual aid society. His admiration is tangible.

Commercial, intensive market gardening was practised in many provincial cities as well as in Paris. One of the most unusual and also most ancient establishments still survives at Amiens. This is a community of some 125,000 inhabitants in the northern province of Picardy. On its eastern edge lie over three hundred hectares of garden plots, a long triangle set in a

The unique water gardens – hortillonnages – *of Amiens.*

ABOVE: The boats of Amiens' ancient market-garden canals are especially designed to protect the banks.

RIGHT: Intelligent tourism which also respects privacy – this is the aim at the hortillonnages *today.*

labyrinth of canals: these are the famous *hortillonnages*. Vegetables were already grown here in the time of Julius Caesar to provide food for Roman soldiers, who called the gardeners *hortulani* (a derivative of *hortus*, meaning 'garden'). Today's market gardeners still go by the name of *hortillons*. Their domain is so unusual that the French government proposed it for inclusion in Unesco's list of sites worth preserving world-wide.

The *hortillonnages* are a man-made landscape: peat cutters extracting fuel long before Caesar's arrival created deep gorges in the Somme and Avre river bogs which eventually became a web of canals. The land they enclosed, a mixture of peat and alluvial deposits, proved ideal for cultivation. But constant human effort has always been required to separate earth from water, keeping the gardens from eroding and the canals from filling up with mud. For centuries, market gardeners spent the winter months on this arduous task. Today there are still over fifty kilometres of canals to maintain – about eighteen of public waterways, the rest private.

These are not allotments, insofar as the land belongs to individual private owners, not an association or the municipality. Fewer than ten market gardeners remain. While each has more land than his ancestors, they still work small patches of half a hectare or less, accessible only by boat.

Many of the properties now belong to weekend residents. Some have built holiday homes in various styles and colours – forbidden by regulation and dangerous on shifting land. The presence of these Sunday gardeners is much debated but without them, whole sections of the *hortillonnages* might well have silted up and disappeared. If their lawns strike a false note, quite a few have put in … plots of vegetables.

Several associations have been founded for the protection of the *hortillonnages*, not only to preserve their heritage but to determine a workable future. The most enterprising was created in 1975 by an amiable eccentric, Nisso Pelossoff. Born in Rhodes, a survivor of Auschwitz, Pelossoff came to Amiens as a photographer after the war where he met and married a local woman. He was the first to awaken public concern when a proposed length of motorway threatened the gardens he had

ABOVE AND RIGHT : Consolidating the banks is essential here. Different gardeners find different solutions.

come to cherish. Now his association has a board of twenty-four volunteer members and a membership of 1300 of which forty per cent are garden owners. It provides jobs for twenty-six employees, often young people such as Pascal Goujon, who ferries curious tourists along the canals and is now proud to have a garden here himself.

Monsieur Pelossoff has found ingenious solutions to protect the site and owners' privacy on the one hand, to create an intelligent form of ecological tourism on the other. With help from city and regional administrations, his association has purchased eight barges for visits which reveal to outsiders a small but representative fragment of the vast labyrinth. The boats are electrically operated so as not to damage the banks. At the same time, the association has obtained especially adapted equipment for cleaning the canals, both public and private. It has preserved both the immense cultural heritage of the *hortillonnages*, and their particularly rich range of wildlife.

Indeed, the *hortillonnages* of Amiens provide a wonderful example of symbiosis between nature and culture – always

inextricable on this site. Willows and alders proliferate naturally but are also planted, as wands simply stuck in the canal bed, to provide fast-growing aquatic hedging. Woven willow fencing called *fascines*, like that used in medieval gardens, may indeed prove the best method for consolidating banks in future.

City and country here form part of the same complex ecosystem. The ensemble of the *hortillonnages* acts as a filter which purifies the canal water as it moves through them, and also as a safety valve which has for centuries prevented the centre of Amiens from being flooded in heavy rains. Many turns of the canals reveal the spire of Amiens' vast Gothic cathedral less than a kilometre away. The same meandering waters which encircle beds of cauliflowers surround picturesque houses in the medieval town, the Saint-Leu neighbourhood. The city corporations of Saint-Leu long prospered from the textile industry, using the canals for rinsing and local plants for dyes – woad providing the beautiful Picardy blue.

Legend has it that, in the thirteenth century, a field of artichokes was donated by a couple of *hortillons* for the building of Amiens' celebrated Gothic cathedral. One of its portals depicts the donors wearing the traditional headgear of the market gardeners, who had their own costumes, festivities, proverbs and even jokes. Many of today's common family names can be traced back to medieval records of market gardening, like the Azérondes, descended from the sixteenth-century boat builder Jean Aux Arondes. The *hortillonnages* were also family gardens, each generation handing on techniques and traditions to the next. Until the advent of refrigerated transport in the 1920s, market gardeners regularly packed their barges with fresh vegetables for the water market of the Oxtail canal (*Queue de vache*), next to the cathedral. This colourful display is now re-created every June as a festival.

City expansion gradually reduced the area cultivated by these families – first the creation of sixteenth-century fortifications, then a broad canal in 1825, later the railway and new arteries for road traffic. Today however the *hortillonnages* have become a new source of pride for the townspeople. The lessons the site can offer are only beginning to be understood. Another association has transformed a former country inn on L'Ile aux Fagots, one of those which used to delight Sunday trippers and boaters, into a conservation centre. Here workshops are available for schoolchildren so they may master, among much else, the art of growing vegetables.

The children, along with the fifty thousand-odd visitors who annually explore the site, also learn why the thirty-foot, flat-bottomed boats have a raised stern (to provide a solid deck for poling) and a raised, elongated bow (designed to avoid damaging the banks and to provide a bridge for landing); how gardeners once transported horse manure delivered by local farmers to peripheral docks, or mushroom compost from abandoned quarries, to fertilize their soil. They also come to recognize the unusual variety of wild flora and fauna that thrive around the beds of carrots and turnips: comfrey, lysimachia, yellow flag, purple loosetrife, firewort, meadowsweet, meadow rue, various cresses, mints, reeds and even wild orchids. Many kinds of fish spawn here – twice the

national average for a comparable area, according to one study which attributes this phenomenon to the dense network of welcoming banks. At least sixty species of birds nest here also, and many take a short rest while migrating – wrens, finches, jays, thrushes, blackbirds and even nightingales, as well as herons, cranes, cormorants and many kinds of ducks.

Ecological symbiosis takes some managing, however. Canal cleaning is now timed to respect the life cycles of both fish and birds. And even so there are problems. The gardeners of Amiens have learned that moles can swim, that coots love to eat tiny hearts of young lettuce, while musk-rats prefer the roots of young cauliflowers. *Ragondins*, or coypu, make holes in their banks and both eat and dig most destructively. To limit their numbers, government agents now give them a pill which sterilizes them for a few years.

Then there are the mallards which nest in full view of passing barges and get fed by tourists. Their population also increases too fast and, while the fully wild ones do not molest growing vegetables, the half-domesticated ones are a pest. The former are transported to other sites, the latter end up on the table of charitable institutions.

All of the support groups concerned with the preservation of this site agree that its principal vocation must remain gardening, but wonder who will work this land in the future. Some nurserymen have recently set up businesses here, specializing in small fruit like raspberries and currants. Professionals and amateurs continue to cohabit. Both now participate in the *Berges fleuries* competition, which encourages them to maintain and even decorate their banks. Young Pascal Goujon, the ferryman, is competing using only native plants, though he has not yet had time to build a toolshed and stores his supplies, for the moment, in a recycled telephone booth...

The remaining market gardeners hope to obtain a special label of quality for their produce. Jean-Louis Christen, gardening on about two hectares all told, has already won the prestigious *Nature et progrès* label for his organic vegetables. The French magazine *Rustica* appeals to public-spirited buyers to purchase unused plots and let them as allotment gardens. All parties agree today on the importance of *hortillonnages* for the community at large.

Michel Serres in his essay *Le Contrat naturel* (The Natural Contract) describes the traditional peasant and sailor as figures whose lives depended, hour by hour, on the sky and the seasons. We need to remember what they knew, says the philosopher, from their most rudimentary techniques to their highest refinements. Sites like the *hortillonnages* of Amiens can serve to enrich both those who live poised between sky, water and land, and those who come there to discover what has nearly been lost.

The hortillonnages *magically blend water, earth, sky, wildlife … and gardens.*

JARDINS FAMILIAUX OF TOURS

Tours has many beautiful urban allotments. In a suburb township inappropriately called Riche, a community association imposes a colourful shed type painted burnt orange, complemented by green or sometimes turquoise trellises for picturesque effect. A sign points to the spot where members can pick up their paint. One of the most harmonious ensembles lies by the seventeenth-century convent of Les Minimes, in what used to be a hospital garden. There was once a stone pillared gate to this walled enclosure but a truck backed into it years ago, and it has never been repaired. The area is definitely private property, but the occasional visitor will be shown prize plants such as a beautiful, spicy-scented apricot rose grown as a standard, or a swath of blue penstemon mixed with pink Salvia horminum. Monsieur Françoise, president of the local association, says he also has a villa in town with a garden but comes here to be with his friends. In another part of the Tours complex, a café-bar and restaurant keeps a special meeting room for the gardeners.

Asians and old France at Alençon

On the edge of the bustling Norman city of Alençon survives a vestige of old France, the Château de Saint-Paterne. Its prosperity depends today on the communal efforts of two clans: the French aristocratic family which has owned it for generations, and an Asian tribe which grows vegetables on its grounds. The French family's heritage is thus maintained, and an immigrant community is able to preserve its own customs.

As a Chinese proverb would have it: 'Life begins the day you start a garden.' Charles-Henri de Valbray was above all intent on maintaining the family estate against encroaching water towers, high-rises and a Moulinex factory for which a large piece of his land was expropriated in 1962. He had already transformed the main wing of his château into elegant *chambres d'hôte,* the French equivalent of bed and breakfast.

ABOVE : At the Château de Saint-Paterne, Hmong gardeners grow vegetables unfamiliar to French neighbours … even sweet-corn.

RIGHT : The Asian patriarch Ly Gé stands among a sea of squashes in the château park.

Then one day in 1991 he saw Asian families filling their baskets in the produce department of the local supermarket and impulsively offered to let them garden a piece of his six-hectare park. The experiment has been hugely satisfactory to both parties, and guests at the Château de Saint-Paterne today eat home-grown vegetables.

A charming young bachelor in his thirties, full of smiles and civilities, Charles-Henri does the cooking and maintenance himself. When Saint-Paterne's park was first diminished in 1962, his father moved to Sanary in Provence, where he bought a flower farm and made his living producing cut flowers and bedding plants. The brother has undertaken the restoration of the Château des Briottières in the Sarthe. Charles-Henri's only help is a somewhat maternal housekeeper, Marie-Louise, who anxiously tries to keep up with the young man's imaginative reorganization.

The Asians, for their part, belong to the nomadic Hmong tribes. They lived for twenty years in Laos before moving to Thailand and thence to France as political refugees. The garden at Saint-Paterne feeds four families of six or seven people each, under the rule of the patriarch Ly Gé. Only one daughter-in-law is fluent in French, and is also one of the few women who has learned to drive. Many seeds and even tools, such as a short-handled, fan-shaped hoe, have been sent from south-east Asia. This Hmong community is Christian, belonging to the Protestant church; but when the former patriarch died, a new garden shed was constructed on the other side to leave the original site free for his ghost.

The Asian potager is visible from the château windows as a kind of froth of floral colour on the south-west horizon, protected by the tall maples and oaks of the park beyond. But it is broad enough to get sunshine and thrive in spite of root competition from these trees. Close up, it has many typical features of allotment gardens all over the country: the cobalt blue plastic water containers; makeshift constructions of recycled planks and boards that, converted into picnic tables, a barbecue and storage shed, achieve a certain elegance of their own.

Some parts are laid out on a grand scale – a mini-meadow of rambling cucurbits and a village of bean poles. Many grow

The Asian vegetable garden is just visible from the windows of the Château de Saint-Paterne, which in turn provides an elegant backdrop for the colourful plantings.

into high blocks: a stand of sweet-corn has been interplanted with more cucurbits which use the tall stems for support. Annual flowers, lettuce and radishes fill in between the rows at the beginning of the season. Every inch of space is put to good use. In other parts of the garden, small plantings intermingle – chives and mint, coriander (sometimes called Chinese parsley) and edible garland chrysanthemums pop up here and there. There are many varieties of onion, garlic and chives, several kinds of oriental cabbage and hot peppers, dwarf and pole beans – including the ones called 'yard-long'. Some plants remain mysterious, since the Asian gardeners cannot communicate their names and locals have rarely if ever encountered them: Charles-Henri has identified one edible flower much prized by the Hmongs as a kind of meadowsweet.

Frost protection, as in other community gardens, mixes tradition and personal ingenuity. Early spring salads are covered with a tunnel of supple, woven branches. Tiny pumpkins thrive under temporary teepees of clear plastic, held in place by rocks. These aids remain useful – and visible – for only a short time in spring; very soon the entire garden ripens into a dense luxuriance entirely hiding the rich, dark brown earth. Charles-Henri claims, with glowing pride, that vegetables grown here are twice as big as elsewhere. He is intrigued by the spicy dishes prepared by the Asian families who even have a favourite sauce using the tendrils of squash plants.

The Hmong community is very close-knit, and Charles-Henri observes without meddling. For many months, a small village of poultry-houses – on stilts, Asian style – flourished in the shelter of the park's tall trees, a highly unusual and picturesque conglomeration for lower Normandy. It contained perhaps a high percentage of large and aggressive roosters of a race little known in France ... but suddenly, overnight, they all disappeared. Had there been a gypsy raid, as neighbours claimed? Intertribal disputes within the community? Today more ordinary brown hens are kept mainly for laying.

No money changes hand between the French scion and the Asian patriarch. The basis of their agreement is barter. The tenants supply vegetables and flowers for bouquets, chickens and eggs in exchange for the land. Charles-Henri assists in other ways when he can, and has even managed to help some of his tenants find jobs in the area. They too add extras: grain for his '*poupoules*' – which is what the Asians call the latest addition to the château park: three peacocks – not very musical, and certainly not to be eaten. (Olivier de Serres said of his that they had angels' wings and devils' voices.)

Neither Charles-Henri nor Ly Gé speaks the other's language, of course. All negotiations are carried on in two modes: gesture and laughter. When the local prefect received two fine pigs as a gift after an agricultural show, he gave them to Charles-Henri who entrusted them to his Asian tenants. As they grow, the two men must decide at what size they will be butchered. Discussion takes the form of stretched palms, rolling eyes, and gales of infectious giggling, during which each observes the other shrewdly but with obvious respect. A few international terms such as 'Kaput!' serve in extreme cases.

On the other side of the road, another park fragment survives which Charles-Henri hopes to transform into a col-lection of rare fruit varieties. He has invited townspeople to donate trees, as a means of involving them in his projects, and gaining their support to protest against the building of a supermarket on this spot. The Château de Saint-Paterne now hosts garden shows, concerts, even small theatrical productions. Perhaps in a year or so one of the outbuildings will be cleared and transformed into a small restaurant serving only one or two dishes daily, based on produce from the estate.

Existence is precarious, but ideas and projects tumble out of the young man's fertile mind faster than it takes to grow Chinese chives. He enjoys it all thoroughly. Meanwhile in the park of Saint-Paterne he and his Asian guests have achieved a rare synthesis between the urban allotment model and gracious country living, between different social classes and even different nationalities. In this, the gardens of Saint-Paterne join a whole new trend in French vegetable gardening which forges new links between city and country life, often moving towards communitarian, even Utopian ideals.

DREAMS AND UTOPIAS

Every gardener today would sympathize with that allotment owner who said, 'My patch is just a little corner of paradise'. Or with his friend, who expressed ever-renewed amazement at the miracle of the sprouting seed. Or with the one who evoked his pleasure in being the first to eat, season by season, the fruits of his garden, taking a raw bite of the first radish, tomato or young cabbage as he walked through his very own plot. Even scholars today publish volume after volume with titles such as *The Garden: Art and Place of Remembrance* or *The Gardens of Homecoming,* so many attempts to circumscribe the imaginative dimension of gardening – dream, memory, projection, idealization. As for the poets, Marie Rouanet says it all in the title of her slim volume, *Tout jardin est Eden* (Every Garden is Eden).

Dreams and Utopias proliferated, of course, during the back-to-nature movement in the 1970s. At that time, writer Pierre Gascar expressed a vision shared by many when he described the idyllic garden he cultivated for years at the Abbaye de Baume-les-Messieurs in the Jura. Here there was no notion whatever of formal designs and square beds, however symbolic. Everything was riotous profusion – small-scale and enclosed, full of a wide variety of simple (single-flowered) common plants. This hymn to creation concentrated on sensuous pleasure – the buzzing of bees, the wafting of scents on summer air.

In this setting, Gascar sought communion with the earth. No mastery of nature here: 'The beauty of the whole... belongs to the delights of disorder', he wrote. Its flora also depended on chance – seeds brought by the wind, or cuttings from neighbours. In such a garden, all sorts of fauna also felt at home. Pierre Gascar entitled his vision of earthy delights *Le Jardin de curé*, or country priest's garden. For the writer, the presence of a man of God implied 'a good-natured devotion to all that the earth produces'.

In France today, the fervour surrounding potagers has promoted more than ever the phrase and the image of the *jardin de curé*. Where does it come from and what does it mean some twenty years later?

St Fiacre, patron saint of gardeners, is still gaining ground today...

The *jardin de curé*

Novelist Michel Tournier and researcher Georges Herscher explored the roots and range of this fashion in a recent book on the subject. In his introduction, Herscher describes a typical Parisian dinner party conversation: 'You have a garden at your country place?' 'Oh, it's just a *jardin de curé!*' 'I'm sure you are much too modest, it must be lovely.' If the conversation goes any further, says the author, both parties will conjure up intimate, walled spaces where flowers, vegetables, herbs and fruit intermingle.

In the same volume, garden writer Jean-Paul Collaert analyses the current *jardin de curé* fashion with recommendations on how best to achieve it. He warns against the confusion, common in the popular press, between old-fashioned French vicarage gardens and English cottage gardens, pointing out that the first always involve a formal layout with paths in a cross design, and not at all the vague exuberance which many people today associate with the image. The authentic *jardin de curé*, Collaert insists, was always, throughout the nineteenth century, a garden of lines, not dabs of colour, though he adds that perhaps due to lack of maintenance the formal geometries might at times be blurred.

Most people today do, however, imagine dabs rather than lines – Delacroix, not Ingres. Or rather the minor nineteenth-century genre paintings which depict various *curés* in their gardens, either meditating by themselves, or with parishioners in need of help. There is a definite anecdotal dimension to these portrayals, a moment of charged emotion, a strong load of sentimental intensity. Formal garden design is absent from these popular visions of country priests in idyllic settings. On the contrary, there is a profusion of colour, definitely dabs and not lines. Could it be that our contemporary image of the *jardin de curé* derives not from the social reality, but directly from these minor sentimental genres of pictorial art?

By the mid-nineties, this vision has conquered even French railway employees, always active and enterprising gardeners. The fiftieth anniversary issue of their gardening magazine uses the term *jardin de curé* to cover several current fashions all mixed together: gardens expressive of individual creativity, full of fragrance, bees, birds and butterflies, surrounded by rustic mixed hedges, leaning towards a less domesticated version of nature. Today, says the editorial, you can grow a wildflower meadow instead of a lawn, plant artichokes among dwarf roses, and maintain a patch of nettles to make plant sprays, without your neighbours looking askance.

The appeal of this dream, even if it springs from fancy rather than social realities, is easy to understand: for most gardeners, it means gardening in amiable partnership with nature, involving neither mastery nor subjection. Hence the disappearance of geometry from the image, removing any connotations of the neo-classical parterre *à la française*.

The nineteenth-century genre paintings of country priests in their gardens were certainly influenced, in their turn, by two writers whose idyllic descriptions of small, exuberant gardens inspired the whole Romantic generation: Bernardin de St Pierre and Jean-Jacques Rousseau. The latter proved especially influential through the paradise garden he imagined for the heroine of his novel *Julie ou la Nouvelle Héloïse*.

The famous orchard-garden Rousseau conceived for Julie is above all an embodiment of desire, memory, emotion. It is a refuge for reverie – humble, small-scale and intimate. It is economical, not extravagant. Here too, plant varieties are not horticultural rarities but common, even wild ones, 'arranged and united in the manner most likely to produce an amiable and charming impression'. Symmetry is definitely banished here as 'the enemy of nature and variety'. Nothing is straight, nothing levelled: 'the sinuosities in their feigned irregularity are laid out with art'. All the senses are solicited in turn. Wild fauna, particularly birds, are welcomed and indeed much effort is expended to recreate their natural habitat so that they will feel at home. There is edible fruit everywhere. The hedge is a rustic one of mixed essences, much like those which nurseryman Dominique Soltner made fashionable again in the 1980s. All has an air of natural, gentle disorder. What could be more like today's dream of the *jardin de curé*?

Rousseau's vision is dated today in one respect: the productive potager on this estate lies outside Julie's garden. If it

too, stipulates Rousseau, 'pleases the eye', it nonetheless still requires cultivation in rows. Today's romantic gardeners put the potager right in the heart of the garden, and often make it the dream's main focus. Around it, they strike a personal balance between formality and gentle disorder, lines and dabs. Edible produce remains essential to the genre, but feeling and mood clearly count more than productivity. 'All that sustains the imagination also excites the mind and nourishes the spirit' – thus speaks the prophetic philosopher.

Nineteenth-century depictions of le jardin de curé *have contributed much to contemporary dreams. Etienne-Prosper Berne-Bellecour,* Le Jardin de M. le curé, *1875.*

Rousseau's ghost at the Château de Mongenan near Bordeaux

In *La Nouvelle Héloïse*, Rousseau also asks, 'How should the man of taste, who seeks only simple and genuine pleasures, plan a walk at the very door of his house? He must make it so convenient and agreeable that he can enjoy it at every hour of the day.' Antoine de Gascq, Baron de Portets, was such a man – one of the best musicians of his time, founder of the Académie de Musique de Bordeaux, president of the Parlement de Guyenne, and friend of Jean-Jacques. Gascq first met the writer when he became Rousseau's music pupil in Paris in 1741. That summer, Rousseau spent some time at Mongenan at the elegant '*folie*' which Gascq had built in 1736 among the vineyards of the prestigious Graves region. The visitor helped his host create an intimate, semi-enclosed garden, delightful indeed at all hours, mingling vegetables, fruit, herbs and flowers. Today this garden is tended and cherished by two of Gascq's descendants, a spirited mother and daughter team, Suzanne Faivre-Mangou and Florence Mothe. The mother made her place in the strongly male-orientated wine community as a vintner as early as 1936; the latter has established herself as an author and journalist in the twin realms of gardens and gastronomy.

Gascq's entire domain was from the start imagined as a kind of self-sufficient Utopian community in miniature, with its well in the courtyard, its dovecote and a small attached farmhouse with room for a pig, some chickens and rabbits,

The walled, sunken garden at the foot of the elegant Château de Mongenan near Bordeaux owes much to Jean-Jacques Rousseau, echoing in many respects the philosopher's idyllic garden in his novel Julie ou la Nouvelle Héloïse.

ABOVE : Pink lavatera intermingle with cabbage and beans near an artichoke plant at Mongenan.

RIGHT : The elegant eighteenth-century garden gate is decked with Paul's Scarlet Climber roses on both sides.

and a bread oven. Around the rest of the house, an English style park was laid out to set off a monumental cedar of Lebanon, planted at the time the *folie* was built. The River Garonne gleams in the sunlight beyond the château's vineyards, bordering the park. Gascq's son, Antoine de Valdec de Lessart, was if anything an even more fervent idealist and disciple of Rousseau than his father. He later achieved prominence as a minister of Louis XVI and director of the Compagnie des Indes, a Utopian economist, Freemason and avid botanist. The small museum of eighteenth-century everyday life now housed in the farm buildings contains his own and also another period herbarium, precious documents for tracing the evolution of plant populations in the area.

Rousseau had yet to write his famous description of Julie's garden when he came to Mongenan as a heartsore young man. But already here, as in Julie's imaginary orchard some twenty years later, the garden is a secret space inviting intimate discovery though situated right 'at the door of the house'. It is designed neither as an extension of the façade nor as an ostentatious promenade but remains hidden, a sunken garden on a lower level, behind a high gate. From the garden, the château's stately proportions can be seen rising above the profusion of fragrant and colourful plants, a reminder of both history and the household connection. In all other respects, the garden remains a world of its own, open only to the sky, its horizons set by the ragged patterns of mimosa and Judas trees in big clumps, and a high wall draped with climbers and tall flowers along the road.

The potager at Mongenan is not a wild space, even less a natural wood, for the basic rectangle remains securely domestic, the beds formally laid out. But all geometry has long been obscured by an indescribable luxuriance. The centre path peters out before the end, and there is no general design readable from any given point. Some of the long, narrow beds run east-west, others north-south. Whatever pattern may appear keeps evolving, in a series of small corners and spaces. 'The taste for distant perspectives comes from the tendency most men possess to be happy only somewhere else than where they are', wrote Rousseau, again praising Julie's garden. 'Here one is very happy without viewpoints for all the charms of nature are enclosed within.'

Each part of the garden at Mongenan is enclosed by green and growing curtains made of espaliered fruit trees, rambling roses and hedges of runner beans, which allow transparency while preserving mystery – one can peek through and over them. But plants often extend also as arches over the paths so that one passes 'under a roof of flowers' as in Julie's garden. The rose, which Julie calls the queen of flowers, 'everywhere shines' here, whether as a La Folette over the entry, a Mermaid draped on wires, a Paul's Scarlet Climber ranging into an old pear tree, or a Souvenir de la Malmaison flowering in this climate until January. Spaces are small and crowded, separated by narrow paths, all very much on a human scale. Everything here is hand-cultivated. Here as with Julie, nature seems to do all ... but is artfully aided by the careful attention of Florence and her occasional helpers. Here as there, wildlife is welcome: birds make themselves at home, and there is a special section planted to attract bees.

The major difference here of course is the presence of vegetables. Here the potager has been integrated into the heart of the maze. A typical bed contains two parallel rows of five Savoy cabbages each at the foot of a fluffy pink hibiscus. Next door, six tomato teepees tower over pickling cucumbers running at their feet. Behind and perpendicular to these run two strips of three rows of fat, shiny-leafed sorrel. Bands of strawberries may be found bordering beds throughout the garden. Many plots, but by no means all, have an edging of Sweet William, or iris or valerian, tufts of gaura or asters.

Mongenan also pays homage to Rousseau's other love, the pursuit of botany. Most of the plants, whether rare or commonplace, are labelled with family and place of origin: *Hesperis matronalis*, example, is listed as a crucifer from East Asia. In some parts of the garden, plants are grouped by family, or by theme. Those used in everyday life in the eighteenth century, for example: saponaria for making soaps; poisons like ricin, aconite and datura which were used for pharmaceutical preparations and other more benign herbs such as mullein or eupatoria; iris which ground into powder served for dressing wigs as well as a treatment for toothache. Medicinal herbs appear all over the garden however: comfrey which was used to heal wounds, thyme, lemon balm, a whole row of angelica, wormwood, rue, lavender, savory, and horse-radish. Botany excuses the presence of exotic plants which Julie shunned: ginger occupies one bed. Perfectly hardy, says Florence Mothe, it thrives if planted vertically, otherwise is likely to sulk and die.

This garden is beautiful in all seasons, but its spring metamorphoses move from the golden mimosas through waves of iris, to the billowing pink of the Judas trees, and on to the roses' main display. In summer, blue and yellow dominate the composition – for here too, art directs nature, and Florence keeps watch on her colour compositions. Dahlias, asters and many varieties of shrubby sage light up the autumn.

This is obviously a much-loved garden, where imagination and sensuality continue to reign in harmony. But if Rousseau is the presiding deity, there is perhaps also another inspiration, having to do with the evolution of the local landscape in the Graves vineyards since World War II.

Both mother and daughter know intimately every feature of the earth their family has cultivated for so many generations. The Château de Mongenan stands on land where wine was already being produced in the third century – though the Romans thought snail-farming more important in this region! The landscape remained much the same for centuries, through many crises of weather and politics, until the fatal year of 1956 when killer frosts destroyed almost everything growing. Until that time, livestock rearing was at least as important here as wine production. Above all, the vines were part of a mixed fabric of vegetables, fruits and grain crops. In her memoirs as transcribed by her daughter, Madame Faivre-Mangou recalls, 'My childhood was cradled by humble visions of turnips, swedes and Jerusalem artichokes covering thousands of acres...' The vines were allowed to layer and climb, creating 'that charming medieval disorder composed by the entanglement of strawberries, asparagus, peas, peaches, almond and lucerne, among the Merlot, Malbec and Cabernet vinestocks.' For hundreds of years, fruit trees stood among the vines as they had done in the Roman era, some varieties brought by the English in the Middle Ages: the Mouille-Bouche (mouth-wetting) pears of the Saint Macaire canton, the Beurré-Clairgeau of Carbon-Blanc, the Rose de Benauge nicknamed *pommes Dieu* (God's apples), or the peaches known as Tétons de Vénus (Venus' nipples). All of this rich agricultural texture remained unchanged until 1956.

But after the devastation of that fatal year, the landscape was regraded, redesigned, laid out in even rows of vinestocks trained on wires, uniform, symmetrical. Polyculture disappeared. Rousseau had praised Julie's garden because it contained 'nothing aligned, nothing levelled,' but modern, machinery-operated agriculture left no room for romantic sentiment. The garden at Mongenan owes much to Rousseau, but perhaps as much to this other, much more recently lost heritage. Part of Mongenan's vocation today is the preservation of old vegetable and fruit varieties – for example the fragrant strawberry called Belle de Bordeaux. The green curtains which separate its garden into compartments may echo not only the secret spaces of Julie's garden but also the trailing and climbing vines and fruit trees that once spread over the hills of the Graves region.

And yet, however nostalgic the vision at Mongenan, there is a place also for hard-nosed practicality. Florence Mothe's books make specific recommendations on the economic and agricultural problems of her region today, looking to promote future well-being which builds on the past. On a more individual basis, she organizes practical gardening workshops to pass on both techniques and the plant lore she knows so well. Best of all perhaps for someone who lives in daily contact with the spirit of Jean-Jacques Rousseau, she has kept her sense of humour. Her two cats are named Monsieur Figaro and Emile. The latter, she explains, recalling the philosopher's treatise on education by this name, because he has been very badly brought up...

A sunlit Savoy cabbage.

The mystic smith of Wy-dit-Joli-Village near Paris

The *jardin de curé* dream, invented by writers and painters, serves in turn as a source of inspiration for other artists, whose creations can be very diverse. One such individual, Claude Pigeard, found his medium in the forging of zinc, tin and iron – and in the garden he created around an old vicarage, which has excited much admiration in recent years.

West of Paris stretch rolling hills so admired in distant centuries that the very town names include the adjective 'pretty'. Close to Mantes-la-Jolie lies the small community of Wy-dit-Joli-Village, 'Wy called pretty village'. Across from its harmonious Romanesque church, where a narrow street opens on to the main road, a high, beige stucco and stone wall bears an inscription: 'Medieval Forge; Gallo-Roman Baths; Tool Museum; Folk Arts and Traditions'. The entrance to this eclectic assembly of curiosities passes under a porch between two houses – the forge, ten thousand tools and the Roman excavations lie on the left, while the house to the right of the entrance passage contains a densely packed exhibit of rustic furniture, pottery, and oddments of all sorts. This is the domain of a passionate collector, whose head is as crammed with information as his buildings are with objects – a careful selection from different periods and contexts, so closely assembled however as to produce an almost surreal juxtaposition. Nor are all of them old, for Monsieur Pigeard is an active smith, working with private customers as well as with the Ministère des Monuments Historiques, to produce everything from shop signs to weather vanes to plant labels (in zinc, using nineteenth-century techniques). His garden is full of these creations, often painted Pompeii red, peacock blue or black – a statue of St Fiacre (patron of vegetable gardeners), plant stakes and supports, and a high, elegant pergola running the length of his garden.

LEFT : In just a few years, Claude Pigeard created a luxuriant profusion of intimate spaces, full of flowers like this rambling Toby Tristam rose.

RIGHT : Trained as a blacksmith, Pigeard makes all his own metal fixtures, labels and plant supports.

ABOVE : Pigeard's garden, witty as well as beautiful, features a cemetery of dead plants. The assemblage of pots and his own labels makes this an attractive arrangement.

LEFT : Profiled behind this exuberance is the house where Pigeard was born, the local vicarage.

ABOVE : On the house wall, Chasselas de Fontainebleau vines next to a door deliberately kept weathered.

RIGHT : Connecting paths remain orderly, in the vegetable plot as elsewhere.

For the gateway museums, which can take hours to explore, are just the beginning. Through the arch can be glimpsed a broad, open courtyard. Here the drive circles a wedge-shaped lawn punctuated with small box balls, the plainest, most formal space of the whole property. On the right stands the eighteenth-century vicarage, the house where Monsieur Pigeard was born and where his mother now lives. Straight ahead and on the left is the main garden, most of it raised a few metres above the level of the courtyard, supported by two stone vaults and reached by a short flight of steps.

In 1968, Monsieur Pigeard was employed at the Renault works near Paris. Following the May 'events', he left to join a community of artists which included Pissarro's grandson. Soon he was back in his home town, restoring this abandoned property with his own hands. Intrepid and intense, Monsieur Pigeard turned his attention to plants only in 1989 and in five years created this *jardin de curé* – nowhere is the phrase more apt – where dozens of rare varieties of flowers, vegetables and fruit hobnob with humble country friends: single flowered hollyhocks, feverfew, dahlias, zinnias, asters and chrysanthemums, and many old rambling roses. The design is simple, though obscured somewhat by the exuberant profusion of rambling, tumbling plants.

The main, raised garden is hemmed in by high walls south and west, but open and looking down over the courtyard to the north and east. It is divided lengthwise by a central path, accentuated for most of its length by the black pergola, supporting rambling roses such as Toby Tristam and Veilchenblau, intermingled with various clematis. To the right of this central axis lie a whole series of box-edged rectangles of different dimensions, included a cutting garden – and the potager. To the left is a medieval-inspired herb garden, a tapestry of aromatics laid out around an iron cross.

In the potager section, very low-pruned apple cordons surround tiny vegetable plots: Cox's Orange Pippin, Ontario Reinette and, appropriately, an old variety called Joli Bois, the fruit of which can be kept for up to two years in hay. Monsieur Pigeard grows enough vegetables to feed his family, but gives full rein both to his collector's passion and his decorator's eye:

Aster horizontalis intermingles with red sorrel and red orach. Good King Henry thrives next to ground-nut. Peruvian physalis (also called Cape gooseberry or goldenberry) rises beyond a bed of multicoloured lettuce edged with perennial leeks. And if flowers spill over among the vegetables, the latter infiltrate the ornamental beds as well: along a north wall, a high stand of Jerusalem artichokes with golden daisy flowers is flanked by pale blue asters, both kept from falling over by a Pompeii red metal support.

The herb garden is more open – in part because the plants are mostly lower-growing, and spaced so that the design of its eight beds remains clearer. But it comes as a surprise, only visible as you emerge from the pergola. Monsieur Pigeard was inspired here by the medieval tradition of gardens as secret spaces which must be discovered by a sort of quest. Here the high back wall supports a medlar, and a bladder senna (*Colutea arborescens*). And here too commonplace aromatics such as rosemary and thyme mix with somewhat rarer lemon balm, true valerian and curled-leafed tansy. Annuals such as corn cockles and Persian Jewels love-in-a-mist add bright accents. It is here that the statue of St Fiacre presides, set on a staff above the globes of the earth, sun and moon.

From the herb garden one can see clearly the eighteenth-century sundial on the main house façade, and the three Chasselas vines pruned to outline its door and windows; the speckled soft rust and grey roofs of the circle of buildings (undulating with age, and restored to remain so); the bell-tower of the church outside; an arbour of trelliswork shading

DREAMS AND UTOPIAS

a table for outdoor meals across the courtyard, and the passage out into the street, where horseshoes hang over the porch.

The colourful abundance of plants is set off not only by Monsieur Pigeard's painted metalwork, but also by terracotta pots of all sizes. Even half-broken ones still serve to display here a tumbling sedum, there a clump of sempervivum. In this garden full of ongoing projects, there is room for chance – a pottery shard falls among the ivy, and remains, for its contrast of colour and texture.

There is also room here for garden virtues which might be more widely appreciated: wit and humour. Just outside the medieval garden, Monsieur Pigeard pays homage to his horticultural failures in a cemetery of dead plants, a grouping of terracotta pots around a small altar. The dry twigs of their mortal remains are barely visible, hidden in a forest of beautiful zinc tags on long spikes, each name commemorating the loss of a loved plant. Elsewhere a mossy stone is inscribed as the bench of St Fiacre, recalling the saint's legendary resting place which retained the imprint of his bottom when he sat on it. A garden tap in the wall is fancifully enclosed in a formal box shape like a foliage fountain. The plant labels and supports often bear playful messages and pictures.

Even more personal is the constant evidence in the garden of Monsieur Pigeard's mystic vocation, as he calls it. Inscriptions can indeed be found all over the garden, and, just as in the much grander gardens of the eighteenth-century philosophers, they generally have a moral import. In one niche, a book (forged from zinc) lies open; on one page can be read condolences for the children of Rwanda, on the other Lafontaine's fable of the Labourer.

Monsieur Pigeard has always been regarded by the townspeople as something of an eccentric. When he talks, he throws his head back, half closes his eyes and pontificates. But not much escapes his glance. He remains good friends with many painters, and more recently musicians, for music promises to be his new passion. Many think he is retired though he is only in his fifties (and his wife has a full time job as a tax inspector). He has no patience with a world which can divide its time between 'work' and 'holiday', 'job' and 'retirement'. From the time he gets up in the morning, takes a cup of coffee to his mother, and then makes his first inspection of the garden, he never has enough time in the day. He welcomes the world to his domain – the film crew for Bertrand Tavernier's *Un dimanche à la campagne* spent three days shooting in this garden. But he is also quite content with the company of his black and white cat Mozart ... and his own unwavering curiosity.

RIGHT : The artist keeps intimate company with his garden, day in, day out.

LEFT : Tomatoes (cherry and full-size) and onions thrive against a low-trained apple cordon, of the Joli Bois variety.

Utopia now

Many idealists of the sixties and seventies participated in the back-to-nature movement, some on family farms, others in Utopian communities, all aiming at self-sufficiency through the production of their own food. In those decades, city life was shunned for healthy country living. Today's idealists are much more radical, seeking to redefine the very definitions of city and country. Many want to create a new harmony beneficial both to nature-starved urban populations and a declining rural economy. Old-time market gardening, suburbia with a difference, provides one important model here. Thus the Jardins de Cocagne movement: cityfolk wanting better produce subscribe and support one or more market gardeners who supply one weekly basket of vegetables per customer, sometimes complete with recipes, delivered to agreed collection

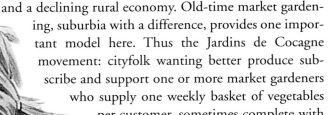

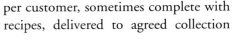

points. First started in Besançon, this movement has now spread to 250 French towns. At Blois, thanks to subsidies and a gift of land from the city, the gardeners are rehabilitated homeless, long-term unemployed and women in difficulty who thus get training to help them find work elsewhere. This endeavour involves support from all levels of administration, however, implying paperwork which can itself be daunting at the outset and funds always in danger of disappearance. Nonetheless the Jardins de Cocagne are proliferating under the banner: 'Cultivating solidarity'.

On a more personal scale, there are couples like Hervé and Jamila Sallé who have spent some years establishing self-sufficient farming near Privas, in the Ardèche. They now organize workshops and experimental gardening for children from underprivileged city neighbourhoods, who thus lose their fear of earthworms, learn to talk to goats and grow their own lettuce. This sort of initiative also has become more and more widespread.

Generally the aim is to promote solid economic exchanges between city people wanting to experience a healthier natural environment and a rural population determined on less industrial methods and better quality produce. Near Grenoble, an association called Citadins-Ruraux uniting small farmers and cityfolk has helped Alain and Yvette Pommard move from market gardening into the production of wheat, flour and organic bread, some of which is sold commercially, some redistributed among association members. The latter come out to the country to help with the work, when, for example, hand weeding is needed to remove wild sorrel from fields of young wheat. The same group has now sponsored a full-time employee to help one of its members, a local sheep farmer.

Important as these social experiments prove to be, it is the small-scale plot rather than agricultural production which offers the most compelling symbol for most people. But the Utopian potager today, whether cultivated by individuals or entire communities, resembles the *jardin de curé* ideal because of its respect for life in all its forms. As garden expert Claude Aubert wrote as early as 1980, an organic garden is 'not just a place that remains unpolluted. It is a spot where the gardener tries to maintain a good relationship with thousands of living species'. In this respect, naturalist Henri Fabre was an important precursor. His Harmas in Provence, where a magic collection of native plants and herbs supports a great range of local fauna, could be considered an early and influential vision. It is also, still today, a beautiful garden.

Today this ideal is called biodiversity and the perspective is often international, if not global, in a world of shrinking natural resources.

ABOVE AND LEFT : Two plant portraits, original photographs by Denis Brihat, both created by an iron-vanadium toning: the heart of a kiwi-fruit, and the stem of a white onion.

FAR LEFT : De Trébons onion

ABOVE : *Aubergine plants in the Brihat garden are staked on hedgerow bamboos and heavily mulched.*

RIGHT : *Photographer Brihat and his dog Cléopatre resting in his limestone grotto garden.*

An alchemist's workshop: Denis Brihat in Provence

Many of the old-guard Utopians have moved on to other visions, illusions and disillusions, but some continue to imagine new worlds thanks to an inexhaustible personal creativity. One of these is photographer Denis Brihat, a particularly resourceful individual who took root in the country, and turned his dreams into a working reality. He has made a reputation for himself by photographing ... vegetables.

Like many of his generation, he chose southern France as his refuge. Novelist Henri Bosco once described such a haven in Provence in idyllic terms as 'nestled under the terrace, sheltered by high, warm walls but open on to the valley full of brown and blue summits, offering to the rosebushes, the tulips, and even to the stray weeds a well of warm air which smelled all at once of fruit trees, hawthorn and hyssop. Birds twittered among the plums... Nothing was more charming than this garden. It existed in this tiny, sheltered bit of land which had trusted itself to man – just big enough for a soul without worldly ambition, or possessing the genius of retirement.' He might have been describing Brihat's garden in the Luberon.

Brihat first escaped from Paris to move south as long ago as 1958. Some years later, Provence began attracting hosts of 'hippies' moving back to the earth. At about the same time, the international jet set took possession of these particular hilltowns, cubist compositions in limestone set in a tough, scrubby, wild and very beautiful landscape. Brihat watched it all, from his perch on the edge of Bonnieux. He describes himself, using the English phrase, as an 'old timer'.

Local legend depicts him living in a log cabin on the mountain as early as the 1930s but he is not, he says, quite as ageless as that. He did for a while camp at La Clapparède, in a

ABOVE : Denis Brihat's grotto reservoir.

RIGHT : Besides the potager, the Brihats have a half-wild orchard and small vineyard.

cabin of his own making, without electricity or running water, carrying buckets of water from the well to develop his films. He gets along with the '*estrangers*' who have come since – even the bankers, he says, are nice when they are on holiday. He regrets the Provence of Giono and Pagnol, whom he knew, and avoids the Luberon of Peter Mayle, whose first home in Provence was in the next village.

Today, in his sixties, Brihat looks like a genial lumberjack or perhaps a summer Santa Claus. He lives with his wife in a modest house he built himself, tucked under the jutting overhang of a limestone cliff. In the morning he works among his vegetables, in the afternoon in his photo laboratory. In both he performs magic metamorphoses; but while the garden prospers in its 'well of warm air', pot marigolds sown haphazardly among the quinces and green peppers, Brihat's photographs are cool, crystalline images of pure sculpted light. Their subject is invariably the vegetables and flowers of his garden.

Nothing grew under this cliff when Brihat first arrived. Now hedges protect seven separate compartments of vegetables. Brihat rotates his crops on a four year basis, and also practises successive plantings throughout the season. He has tried to use a sprinkler system, but the local water is so full of chalk that the holes plug up in no time. Luckily there is a pretty spring in his cliff wall, which opens into a small grotto. Goldfish live in its reservoir, to keep down mosquitoes.

In a typical year, the first compartment might be given over to early potatoes, including the blue ones which keep coming back as volunteers. They will be followed by mustard grown as a green manure, producing cheerful yellow flowers on dark green foliage even in the heat of summer. Next door, a bright green strip of carrots runs at the foot of a stand of artichokes, which provide beautiful fountains of silvery foliage in winter, but die back fast as soon as the heat arrives. The white rock rising at the back of this garden reverberates heat tremendously, even for Provence.

In the third space, tomatoes, peppers, red cabbage, broccoli and twenty staked aubergine (half grafted on to tomato vines) all live peaceably together, interspersed with lavender. Then leeks (always malingering here, he finds) with celery and strawberries; further on, squash and courgettes, interplanted with potatoes and chard. One more section might be devoted to leguminous crops, peas and a variety of beans including winter keepers. Mustard replaces them as they are picked.

More tomatoes and Golden Bantam maize grow together further along, protected in early spring with old curtains. Beyond, there is a kiwi vine and a stand of bamboo, one variety for edible shoots and another to provide supports for climbing vegetables. Along the side, grow huge tufts of lemon verbena and a row of Jerusalem artichokes flowering in late summer. Unlike many French gardeners who remember living off this hardy vegetable during World War II, Brihat still enjoys eating them.

Besides the open plots, there is a half-troglodyte greenhouse built into the back wall about half way down the garden. Its two stone pillars stand under the rock framing the

Lavender and courgettes – a Provençal potager blend.

become improvised sculpture. Even when reduced to rubble, it had to be carted away bit by bit.

The photographer's close companion for the last quarter-century has been a much-loved van. The slightest trace of rust is carefully treated and removed. It has had to transport all manner of garden supplies from horse manure to loads of earth from nearby Roussillon (brilliantly tinted red and orange and rich with iron) or sand from the Durance river bed. Sometimes Brihat brings back bundles of nettles to make his favourite maceration which, sprayed on foliage, both feeds the plants and controls pests. He also likes to use heather branches to protect young sowings, and these too he must gather elsewhere.

Brihat has widely experimented with compost making, and little piles in various stages of decomposition are neatly arranged in odd corners, covered with canvas. He adds activators bought from the Fubiona company in Roussillon, now famous in the region for its organic products. He also gets manure from his own chickens. And since he loves sweet-corn, he keeps a grinder for the stalks, not one with teeth, he specifies, but one with knives that can chop damp material without seizing up. The end result is used for mulch.

His methods have always been organic. He remembers that in Bonnieux in the 1950s the local peasants were too busy trying to convert to modern agriculture to spend time on family vegetable gardens. They bought their produce from the grocer who obtained it himself from the valley market gardeners. It was plentiful and local, but enriched with industrial fertilizers and covered with sprays. Brihat already then preferred safer and tastier vegetables. Later he discovered the magazine *Les Quatre Saisons du jardinage*, and learned he was not alone. He found it so poetic that he would read it before going to sleep, to inspire his dreams.

One of these was clearly that of Marcel Pagnol's famous hero, Jean de Florette, who announced, 'I want to live in communion with Nature. I want to eat the vegetables of my garden, the oil of my olive trees, to suck the fresh eggs of my chickens, to get drunk on the wine of my vines, and as far as possible to eat the bread I make with my wheat.' Since

broad entrance to a small cave, which will soon receive a glass front. Closer to the house, a low stone ledge also set into the rock wall serves as a planting bed for winter salads. With only a light frost protection, they produce from September to early May, since Brihat keeps harvesting only the outer leaves.

Brihat welcomes some of nature's chance additions, like wild flowers, or a grapevine which cascades down from rock face above. But when a whole piece of the cliff fell, like a meteor, into the heart of his garden, he had to protest. All the more so as the owner of the upper land was slow in paying for the rock's removal – and it had to be broken up with a jackhammer! Brihat's spaces are too tiny for this intruder to

Brihat's space is limited, he mostly grows table grapes though he does make about ten litres of his wine yearly. He also grows wheat, but just enough to harvest wheat germ, which he chews every day in winter. It is to this habit that he attributes his immunity to colds.

Brihat's photographs are hung in New York, Amsterdam, Milan and Moscow, but he prefers to stay at home in his garden. He was invited to New York for a show some years ago, but the only good experience of that trip, he recalls, was letting two squirrels run up his arm while walking in Union Square. After much travel in his youth, including a year in India, he now prefers to journey in imagination.

His pictures certainly penetrate right to the heart of their subjects. Brihat not only develops his films but tints the prints with different metals. Thus uranium gives a look of burnished copper to the inside of a green pepper. Curly endive salad is portrayed with the help of vanadium, silver sulphate and iron. The result is sometimes compared to the poems of Francis Ponge, who also completely removes objects, fruit and vegetables, from their utilitarian context to make them hang mysteriously in space. Like Ponge, Brihat plays with differences of scale – the green pepper becomes an immense cavern. Everyone talks about 'little green men', he says, but they have been here all along, living in a plant civilization parallel to our own, which we must discover and reveal. He treasures the reactions of a village smith to his art years ago: 'I know what that is, but it makes me think of something else.' The aim is to look at nature afresh. This communion with nature, and particularly with vegetables, is the work of a modern alchemist.

A simple and beautiful courgette flower.

Potagers for a small planet: the Domaine de Raud in the Alps

The magazine so much appreciated by Denis Brihat, *Les Quatre Saisons du jardinage*, was founded by three active organic gardeners, Claude Aubert, Jean-Paul Thorez and Karin Mundt. Today, while Thorez has started a magazine of his own, *Nature et jardin*, Aubert and Mundt have found a place of their own, a spot to make their generous dreams come true, the Domaine de Raud.

Raud is a fairytale realm where houses have boots and hats, and all the toads are princes. Here in the French Alps, the staff of *Les Quatre Saisons du jardinage* test different modes for ecologically balanced living before reporting back to their 21,000 very faithful readers. New techniques include building houses with bricks of raw earth, an efficient method as long as the foundations (or 'boots') are of stone and the roofing (the 'hat') waterproof. The result, designed by Jean-Vincent Berlottier of Lyons, is called the Blue House: a sober, elegant, soft-toned construction housing the administrative centre where every important new dream takes shape. Nearby stands the giant, four-hundred-year-old oak which has become the symbol of the group's association, which goes by the name of Terre Vivante (Living Earth).

This is the Triève region, given over largely to pasture land and cereal crops. Writer Jean Giono who spent holidays here in the early thirties described it as 'this high country studded with knolls, ravaged by torrents a hundred metres deep in the shale, surrounded by enormous mountains rising straight up in the air, blue as canyons of the sea'. The Domaine de Raud covers the bottom of a broad valley at a height of about seven

The Domaine de Raud has several experimental potagers. The family one, of two hundred square metres, lies at the bottom of this hill.

ABOVE : Leafy Swiss chard which needs a good supply of nitrogen grows next to beans, which provide it – a good example of companion planting.

RIGHT : The whole Domaine de Raud is a vast clearing in a valley, surrounded by forest and high mountains in the Trièves region.

hundred metres, with an area of some fifty hectares of woods and scrub. It shelters a particularly rich range of wild flora and fauna. Since moving here in 1993, Karin Mundt (publisher, writer, gardener and prime mover) has been discovering new plants almost daily. She speaks with pride of Raud's twenty-two species and two sub-species of orchid. And she has quite fallen in love with the orange-bellied, singing toads. Each one strikes a different tone at sunset.

Les Quatre Saisons du jardinage began appearing on a shoe-string budget in 1980. When its founders decided to set up a centre, many readers proposed sites; some were too close to a nuclear plant or high tension electricity lines, others fraught with problems of local politics. Finally the mayor of the small mountain town of Mens, a subscriber, proposed the Domaine de Raud.

Beginnings were difficult however. Local hunters resented their arrival and one or two may still be removing all the Centre's roadside signs. Worse yet was the discovery that those picturesque knolls admired by Giono are the result of frequent landslides. A project to construct another large building near the potagers has been abandoned as unsafe. There is also a serious lodging problem not only for the staff but for the many volunteers, student helpers, workshop participants and the conscientious objectors who may legally work out their military service here. Triève is not, or not yet, a resort community and temporary housing does not exist. Thus the whole undertaking proved taxing in unexpected ways. But in spite of all these hurdles, in its first three years the Domaine created twenty-six jobs for full-time staff.

The progress made in only three years is quite amazing. The Blue House contains a library specializing in alternative lifestyles, a small shop, editorial offices, and a welcome centre for the public. Within easy walking distance can be found the Table de Raud (a restaurant with excellent food and a Nubian vault of raw earth blocks); the energy centre with both solar and photovoltaic panels and an efficient, high-powered, wood-burning furnace; compost toilets, the waste water of which is purified though a series of carefully controlled and specially planted reed beds; a vast Syrian tent which houses a

permanent exhibit of 'soft' or ecologically sound construction methods; an operative composting centre displaying seven different home models; an imaginative playground for children; a broad, half-cultivated wildflower meadow; an artesian well; a plant nursery; several ponds; a round, solar beehive made of straw mixed with plaster. There are numerous vegetable plots and more are planned.

Landscape architect Gilles Clément, whom Mundt describes as the most ecology-minded of contemporary designers, was invited to help plan the gardens here. Whole sections of the domain, like the Water Walk with its half-natural, half-constructed series of rocks, cascades, and little bridges, recall parts of Clément's own garden (see page 172). Right at the heart of Raud is the Garden of the Five Elements designed by Clément among the ruins of the original stone farm house (wood is the fifth). Here each separate space is enclosed in low, dry-set stone walls. To ensure that traditional methods of rebuilding would be used, Clément donated his designs and even gave two days of his time to work himself among the other volunteers, setting stone on stone with his own hands.

Clément also designed here a whole series of woodland clearing gardens scattered over about forty hectares, not yet implemented. The team at Raud is exploring economic uses of scrubland (or *friche*) for intensive stock raising (saving, when possible, endangered breeds of livestock); for meadow-orchard combinations; for the intensive cultivation of wild herbs and flowers for medicinal purposes, for use as dyes, or to attract bees. Here too Clément's approach of gently shaping and guiding natural vegetation perfectly suits their aims. Maurice Chaudière has contributed an original 'fruit forest'.

The potagers are equally experimental, many and varied, spread out on a broad slope, where trim lines of vegetables circle round the hillside. All the beds are irregularly dovetailed wedges. Says one of the gardeners, 'A potager must make you dream, and this means curves, not those tight squares...'

There is the special garden for pumpkins and other cucurbits; another called 'the hundred-square-metre exploit'; a potager based on the plant associations recommended by Gertrud Franck; a garden for the preservation of endangered heirloom vegetables; another for available but little-known varieties which should be more commonly planted, such as violet carrots, Jerusalem artichokes, swedes, blue potatoes, parsnips, kale, Italian broccoli rab, hyacinth beans, amaranths and red and green orach. Bare spaces fill in quickly with beautiful 'green manures' such as the sky-blue flowered *Phacelia tanacetifolia*, or brilliant yellow mustard. Flowers are everywhere – as companion plants, to attract bees, and to eat in their own right. Split logs outline the beds, and tidy paths are covered with home-shredded bark and wood chips.

One of the most beautiful and informative potagers is the family garden. Neatly organized on only two hundred square metres, it includes not only rows of vegetables but a flowering hedge, a mini-pond stocked with fish, a cutting garden, a shade tree with bird houses, a paved space with a bench offering a mountain view, a small fruit garden, a herb plot, a compost corner with tubs for making nettle and comfrey

ABOVE : *The goldenberry (*Physalis peruviana *var.* edulis*), related to the tomatillo and the popular Chinese lantern, and today much loved by avant-garde chefs.*

LEFT : *The garden shed demonstrates four different types of constuction using earth.*

Highly decorative Swiss chard and vine-ripened tomatoes.

macerations, a strip of wild flowers to bring bees, and a grassy stretch to provide a play area for children. Flowers again pop up everywhere.

And yet gardening is not easy in this high valley. The growing season is short. Wildlife can sometimes be overfriendly – deer, hare, boar still abound here. Many locals made dire predictions about the very alkaline, heavy clay soil. But the seven different types of home composter prove their merit in such circumstances. Nature is gently managed: special German traps catch field mice, while a wide variety of bird houses

attracts helpful species. There is even a nest for hedgehogs.

The Terre Vivante centre approaches the earth as a small and precious planet, but also as a global village. Few communities are more international. Karin Mundt herself is German, but helped set up the International Federation of Organic Agricultural Movements, has worked in Sweden, Kenya, Spain and Japan to mention only a few, and actually learned to get along in all these languages. Among the regulars at Raud today are Jeremy Light from the Centre for Alternative Technology in Wales, Ali from Iran who looks after general maintenance, Farida Rémila, the cook of Algerian origin, an architect from Naples whose many duties have included erecting the vast Syrian tent. The centre's many sponsors are also world-wide, though mostly French and German. Karin scouts far afield in seeking specialists for the centre's workshops: Anne Rigier for example, who rediscovered ancient methods of dyeing cloth with plant juices using lactofermentation instead of boiling. She restores rare carpets for the British Museum and similar institutions. Or a German specialist who creates living buildings from willows. At the same time, the centre works with every level of government, from the LIFE programme of the European Community, to national projects for the promotion of organic agriculture, to regional efforts for the preservation of disappearing varieties of trees, or local efforts for the development of ecological tourism. Thanks to all this activity, the mayor of Mens should now be able to adopt as a motto for his town: *'Mens sana in corpore sano'...*

Raud's magic springs from its creators' gift for maintaining childlike delight in discovering, respecting and promoting the world's infinite diversity. Their feet are in the ground – muddy from working the earth – but they still love to count the stars.

Raud is not an isolated adventure. More and more idealists all over France, as individuals and in groups, are turning to vegetable gardening as a model for social harmony. The sentiments expressed by ethnobotanist Pierre Lieutaghi in 1980, in a long song of praise to the joy of gardening, would be shared by many home adepts in France today: 'The potager provides a model for managing the world ... if we apply there the knowledge we have now acquired about the life of the soil and of plants, along with simple, basic technology, we can easily achieve in it an optimal and durable understanding with the Earth.'

Gilles Clément's beautiful Fire Garden at the Domaine de Raud.

'LE POTAGER D'UN CURIEUX': JEAN-LUC DANNEYROLLES

Jean-Luc Danneyrolles holds court at the Friday morning market in Apt for farmers, housewives, tourists, Japanese television crews and fellow connaisseurs of rare vegetables. In 1985, he says, he discovered love and gardens at the same time. Ten years and four children later, he had set up a six-hectare Provençal farm on eleven small terraces in the Luberon. Here he produces many different kinds of salad, several varieties of physalis, and such unusual tomatoes as the

Téton de Vénus, White Quebec, and the Italian Stallion (or Tigre Vert), given to him by the daughter of Albert Camus. He also offers for sale seeds and dried herbs.

Something of a philosopher, Danneyrolles values biodiversity, seeking to enrich the future by preserving the past. An artist too, he paints his watering cans and decorates his greenhouses with Matisse reproductions. Danneyrolles' reputation is now such that he has been asked to plant kitchen gardens for two highly respected chefs: Reine Sammut in Lourmarin and Alain Ducasse of Monte Carlo, at the latter's country bistro at Moustiers-Sainte-Marie.

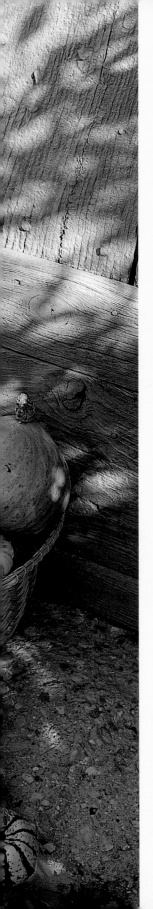

IV

VEGETABLE GRACES

LEFT : *Large Rouen Leek (*Poireau très gros de Rouen, *Vilmorin).*

RIGHT : *Page from the* Larousse Universel, *published in two volumes in 1923.*

PAGE 136 : *At its most perfect, the cabbage becomes a work of art.*

The garden created by Colette at Saint-Tropez in the 1920s is often cited today as a model for elegant earthiness. In planting her retreat, she shunned merely decorative Riviera exotics in favour of beautiful edibles: 'Be calm, my garden, be wise! Remember that you must also feed me ... I want you decked out, but with vegetable graces!' Colette's vision had the power of prophecy: the rustic refinement she celebrated already in that far-off time once more inspires the dreams of sophisticated garden connoisseurs today. The potager has become more than ever before an ideal in which taste as flavour and taste as elegance combine in an exaltation of country charm. Not surprisingly then, style-setters in many domains choose to cultivate vegetables for show, from famous cooks to the best and most ambitious landscape architects. And if fashion, by definition, goes to excess, one may remember chef André Daguin's admonition that a current fad is often the exaggeration of a good idea.

Chefs' creations

Some of France's great chefs were indeed among the first to imagine potagers as show gardens in recent times – designed to create a mood, a décor and as a symbol at least as much as for productivity. Pierre and Jany Gleize, father and son, have long received a cosmopolitan public in their mountain inn at Château-Arnoux in Provence, where Pierre still enjoys cultivating an old-fashioned kitchen garden. Their herb border however is grown largely for display. Like other southerners, they pick herbs wild for cooking because these have a much more pungent flavour. But many guests and even visiting journalists have often never seen sage or thyme growing, and the restaurant garden offers that opportunity more conveniently than a walk in the *garrigue*.

More recently, Provençal chef Alain Ducasse, always at the forefront of fashion, has opened a country inn at Moustiers-Sainte-Marie. Riviera landscape architect Jean Mus created for this Bastide, at the foot of the picturesque medieval hilltown, a formal potager which is arguably the most elegant restaurant garden in France. It contains many rare vegetables, carefully planted by specialist Jean-Luc Danneyrolles. Nothing could better exemplify the current vogue of the French potager than this plot, which represents the efforts of three top experts in both gastronomy and garden design. This is rustic refinement indeed.

LÉGUMES ET PLANTES POTAGÈRES

Pomme de terre saucisse — Quarantaine violette — Panais — Betterave à sucre — Betterave fourragère — Carotte fourragère — Carotte demi longue — Topinambour — Radis rond — Radis long — Carotte ronde — Pomme de terre ronde blanche — Poireau — Épinard — Navet long — Navet plat — Navet rond — Fève — Salsifis noir — Pois mange-tout — Haricot blanc — Lentille — Cresson — Salsifis blanc — Betterave à salade — Pois droit — Oseille — Oignon pyramidal — Pois serpette — Haricot mange-tout — Oignon fond — Oignon plat — Chou d'York — Céleri — Chou de Bruxelles — Céleri-rave — Chou-fleur — Échalote — Chou cœur de bœuf — Asperge — Chou-rave — Ail — Chou de Milan — Chicorée frisée — Mâche — Romaine — Artichaut — Piment long — Scarole — Potiron turban — Aubergine longue — Tomate ronde — Piment carré — Laitue — Melon noir des Carmes — Melon à rames — Melon brodé de Tours — Aubergine ronde — Cornichon — Tomate ordinaire — Melon cantaloup — Pastèque — Potiron géant — Courge à la moelle — Concombre — Pâtisson — Courge sucrière

Millot

Voir BOTANIQUE, FEUILLE, FLEUR, FRUIT, PLANTE.

Jean Bardet's curiosities at Tours

I n the more northerly climate of the Loire valley, chef Jean Bardet makes full use of his beautifully laid out herb garden and of the vast vegetable plot beside it. Jean and Sophie Bardet preside over the Belmont estate on the northern edge of the city of Tours. Their region is famous for its soft, changing light and the splendid châteaux built up and down the river valleys during the Renaissance by French kings, their courtiers – and mistresses. The French spoken here has long been considered a model for its purity and style. Bardet is quick to point out that Touraine differs from other regions in France in having reached beyond a merely local identity to become cosmopolitan centuries ago. The vineyards here contain 'all the vinestocks of the world, and every quality of wine'. If Touraine has often been called the garden of France because of its mild, caressing climate, it is an open garden, says Bardet, not one closed behind high walls.

The Bardet mansion is not Renaissance but Romantic, and was built in the early years of the nineteenth century. In 1810 the main garden lay on the other (west) side of the house, and the working kitchen garden was tucked away out of sight. But today the house has been reorientated towards the east, and

RIGHT : *Like many château potagers, the Bardets' garden spreads round a central pool.*

ABOVE LEFT : One of the many beautiful purple basils.
ABOVE RIGHT : Bronze-leafed mustard.
RIGHT : Jean Bardet's ninteenth-century greenhouse counts among the most elegant survivors of the period.

the large, rectangular vegetable plot has become the heart of the Bardet garden, visible from the dining room terrace and within easy reach of the kitchen. Its elaborate greenhouse was built around 1870.

Along the whole north side of the property grow trees (sequoias and maples) from the original planting, now nearly two hundred years old and giant in their proportions. They make a formidable and competitive backdrop for vegetables, though an unbeatable windbreak. The house and greenhouse to the west, flanked by a formal row of pleached lime trees, help establish proportional balance as well as a further sense of enclosure, while the east and south offer open vistas over grassy promenades beyond.

The Bardets began their garden in this worthy setting in 1989. A landscaper was called in to redesign the grounds and produced something Bardet now feels much too much resembles a public park. He takes a deep personal interest in the whole property, wandering around like any gardener, asking himself if this or that should be pruned or replaced, and

admiring a combination which has turned out just right. Many things do not get done simply because he has no time to do them himself. The ornamental garden is large and well-stocked with trees and shrubs for all seasons, but plants for food production find their way into odd corners. Beyond the swimming pool is a tall trellis arbour supporting the more rambling squash and pumpkin, too voluminous for the main potager. Some fifty varieties of fruit tree have also been planted, including a mixed hedge at the back of the garden with a medlar tree (Bardet nibbles them absentmindedly as he talks), quince, mountain ash and elder, the berries of which go into fritters.

There is even a small vineyard of twelve rows, the vines staked on wires supported by posts made of shale, that dark, metallic stone which provides roof tiles for all the grand châteaux.

The potager, however, remains Bardet's treasure trove, pride and joy. It abounds with rare collector's items, but its arrangement is first meant to please the eye. Its traditional,

Vines here are supported by poles cut from shale, a common local material.

even slightly old-fashioned, appearance suits the nineteenth-century setting admirably: standard roses, dwarf box edging, apple espaliers. Keeping its four-part but not quite symmetrical layout, he built a round basin in the centre, which he decks with nasturiums and fragrant pelargoniums early in the season, followed later by the overflowing foliage of squash plants.

The public is invited to inspect and explore, and indeed this garden is educational and seductive all at once. In 1993, it produced 140 varieties of tomato, a selection reduced in 1994 to only 55 ... including local ones such as the Gardener's Delight (*Délice du jardinier*). Bardet also grows with pride his beautiful 'melon-pear', in fact a kind of aubergine (*Solanum muricatum*), as well as red orach, tuberous oxalis (or 'oca'), and

ground-nuts. He has yet to discover the delights of sweet-corn, however, which he deems good only for rabbits.

Bardet also explores alternative methods of cultivation, favouring the organic approach. He claims that technique can be as important as varietal choice in determining taste; that, for example, all sorts of potatoes can be good depending on how they are grown. He is much interested in current efforts to establish labels of quality for vegetables, like AOC wine.

Touraine's garden image does not usually focus on vegetables, in spite of the proximity of Villandry's famous potager parterres. But the Loire's sandy banks, often very alkaline, produce not only famous wines but the white asparagus of Bourgeuil which Bardet serves with morels. The Bardet potager is the site of a meeting for collectors of rare vegetables every autumn – Victor Renaud, Pierre Bourgois, J-B. Pradet and others well-known to readers of the French gardening press congregate to have tomato tastings, like the wine or olive oil tastings organized by Bardet's colleagues at other famous restaurants.

And yet, if the garden's scientific interest is compelling, its sensuality predominates. It does lie immediately next to the kitchen, and the youngest cook emerges from time to time with a wicker basket to fill up with salads – a blend cut from a tapestry featuring dozens of different varieties of lettuce – and above all with herbs.

The slightly raised herb garden occupies a separate strip along the north edge of the potager, its outline prettily accentuated by borders of bricks laid on their sides. Here grow some twenty-five sorts of thyme, two of giant hyssop (*Agastache rugosa* and *mexicana* from which Bardet makes herb butters), chrysanthemums with mint-flavoured leaves, sweet woodruff which he uses in wine sauces, and much more. '*Tout doit être une cueillette*', says Bardet, 'Everything must make you want to pick and taste.'

The chef transforms his own temptations into seductive dishes: shrimp with broad beans and basil, rabbit with turnips, lamb with broccoli mousse, a mushroom 'symphony' with lovage and the parson's nose (or as the French put it, the bishop's bonnet – the best part of the chicken as any chef will confirm), or a bean terrine, a fricassee of little eels from

Peppers delight the eye as well as the palate.

the Vendée with sage and garlic, tiny mushrooms picked in the vineyards cooked with fresh ginger. One of Bardet's most popular inventions is the vegetable dumpling (*pannequet de légumes*) into which mixed cress and parsley juice is poured just before serving.

Bardet likes to use his herbs fresh, both for smell and flavour. Tarragon and oregano he will admit might be dried, but the very idea of 'bouquet garni' makes him grimace. To keep the best flavour, herbs should be added only ten minutes before the end. Hyssop in chicken broth, just lightly rubbed to release its essence, flavours with a caress. A quince jelly takes on admirable nuances when a few leaves of fragrant pelargonium are wafted through the pot towards the end of its cooking.

Jean Bardet's garden is a projection of his whole expansive personality. His name is everywhere in the establishment, linked with that of his wife and partner, Sophie. In the potager, he works with a well-trained and devoted gardener. Asked what he looks for in a gardener, Bardet answer unhesitatingly, 'Curiosity and poetry'. These are qualities which he himself certainly possesses to a high degree.

And when the bustle gets overwhelming, Bardet has another, purely practical vegetable garden at Vouvray just down the road from Tours, where he takes refuge from time to time to drink a glass of the famous white wine while munching an icicle radish. This is his personal version of the paradise garden...

Sarriette

Basilic

feuil

Persil plat

Christine Guérard's country styles in Aquitaine

The gastronomic establishment most renowned for the sheer elegance of its gardens, however, as both an expression of personal style and a symbol of gracious country living, is the spa hotel Prés d'Eugénie, the domain of Michel and Christine Guérard.

Some twenty years ago, Michel Guérard invented *cuisine minceur*, a refined blend of health and *haute cuisine* that regularly replaced rich sauces with vegetable purées. This turn in his career resulted from his meeting in Paris with a dark, long-haired beauty from the south-west. Michel was floating, Christine had her feet on the ground – indeed rooted in the earth of her native province, her degree from Paris's most prestigious business school notwithstanding. She had inherited a spa at the luxurious resort town of Eugénie-les-Bains (named for the wife of Emperor Louis-Napoleon) and was looking for a first-rate chef. Michel let himself be tempted, wondering if cooking for a spa would be like a return to the privations of the war years. But he found himself in a well-supplied region combining the resources of both the Bordeaux area and gastronomically rich Gascony. A region, says Christine still today, where people think of nothing but eating and festivity, whose earthy cuisine makes the much touted Provençal fare look pale and oversophisticated in comparison. The couple married soon after, and Michel helped transform a place for cures into a centre of earthly delights. Today the resort's advertising compares them to Eleanor of Aquitaine and her troubadour poet-prince.

When Christine took over the establishment, in one corner of the park was an eighteenth-century convent still occupied

LEFT : *Christine Guérard's famous* jardin de curé *largely devoted to herbs and aromatics, very much a show garden.*

ABOVE : The eighteenth-century convent, its stone basin now overflowing with fragrant thyme.

RIGHT : The Guérard style never looks too new, and always combines use with beauty.

by nuns. Alongside, the local curé's father tended a big vegetable garden. The nuns, a teaching order, left in 1968 and the Guérards used the building to store wine until 1987, when they could afford to transform it into a picturesque annexe to the hotel. Christine rejuvenated the old potager by creating her famous and much photographed *jardin de curé*. Today it contains not only beds of fragrant roses but carefully labelled plots of sorrel, chives, parsley, fennel, bush thyme, sage, tarragon, and mint, in a beautifully designed display. Above all, lemon verbena (now called *Aloysia triphylla*) which since childhood has been Christine's signature plant.

For her gardens are rooted in early memories. She recalls the vast park of her family château near Toulouse, where her mother lavished care on her roses and where the potager, in the years just after World War II, was at its most expansive. Such country domains lacked nothing even then – ducks, geese, game, fruit and vegetables, everything cooked and preserved at home in the traditional ways. She remembers with pleasure the strawberries, apricots and half-wild peaches which grew among the vines. And the smell of roses in bloom from April to Christmas, as can happen only in the south. Above all, the thrill of discovering that each day brought its own distinctive harvest, from season to season.

When she was ten, her parents took over the spa at Moltige-les-Bains, in the foothills of the Pyrenees – a dry, scrub landscape full of olive trees and holm oaks, cistus and wild box. Here she and her sisters spent many hours with the two gardeners – one a white Russian called Basil, the other a Spanish 'red' known as Sebastian, always the best of friends in spite of their origins. They took time to teach the three girls to garden, each with a plot of her own. The competition was often fierce.

In Moltige, the potager was cultivated Arab-style, as befits a drier climate, with irrigation canals dug along each row and filled one day a week. Christine remembers village squabbles over water rights. At the same time, because this was a hotel garden, it had to look good at all times. It was kept full of sumptuous flowers for bouquets, and the fruit cordons had patches of lettuce at their feet.

Winter savory, flowering thyme, wormwood and rosemary in the jardin de curé *of Michel and Christine Guérard.*

The nostalgic herb garden which Christine baptized the *jardin de curé* was created in 1989. Since 1993, two new premises have been added at the other side of the town's spa: the Maison Rose and the Ferme aux Grives. The first, a large pleasant building dating from 1830, houses the *cuisine minceur* workshops. The second is an eighteenth- and nineteenth-century farmhouse, beautifully restored in the regional style of Les Landes, with drying maize ears suspended from the roof overhang. The old hay barn has become a restaurant where Michel Guérard presents his version of simple peasant fare – indeed local country folk come here to taste the game on a spit, or *garbure*, the cabbage soup of the region. The main potager grows next to the Ferme aux Grives.

Already in its courtyard, vegetables provide a décor. Visible from the wrought-iron entrance gate are tomato teepees set in brown earth circles surrounded by grass, nasturtiums billowing at their feet. Further on, raised square beds on the warm-toned beige gravel display a mixture of low-growing aromatics, small-scale ground cover roses like Nozomi, strawberries and bright green or rust-coloured lettuce. But the farm's main feature is the formal, tiered potager at the far end of the building, framed by the covered walk linking the house to the old dovecote. It rises on a slope above a low wall of golden stucco and pebbles from the Adour river, topped by urns simply planted with strawberries. Two larger pots containing lavender flank the iron gate. On either side of a central path lined with lemon verbena, moving up long steps held in place by weathered logs, symmetrical rows present cascading nasturtiums, burnt-orange pumpkins, purple-blue leeks, lavender, lettuce of various hues, silver artichokes, lush and fragrant lemon balm, tall aubergine and tomato plants on bamboo supports with more nasturtiums at their feet, and, at the very top, a row of deep red cosmos.

Nothing is rare, everything is cosy and familiar, colourful and comfortable. It is typical of the Guérards' style that nothing ever looks too new, even the most recently created features. This potager is quite unlike any genuine peasant potager, and indeed has no pretensions to being anything but decorative, in which aim it completely succeeds. It aims to complement the picturesque rural architecture much as eighteenth- and nineteenth-century paintings of luscious food add interest to interior settings. Lemon verbena is not Christine's only emblem, moreover, the sign of her directing presence throughout this empire. In every room, a few apples sit in a row on windowsill or fireplace, chosen for colour, shape and taste, the very essence of simple, edible décor.

The Guérard's current project, and now their private residence, is the majestic Château de Bachen a few kilometres from the town. Private in a limited sense only, since many parts are on show on special opening days, especially the reception rooms and the two test kitchens Christine designed for Michel. Even more public is the winery, where wines of the Tursan (already being promoted by Eleanor of Aquitaine in the twelfth century) are today produced by the most modern methods.

If even this family residence has been designed for the public eye, an idyll to be imitated, what constitutes Christine's secret garden today? To one side of the château's stately oak avenue lies yet another potager – surely the simplest, most private patch of the entire estate. Nothing here is intended for visitors. It is a simple series of beds sporting six tomato towers, a square of salads, a few courgette and cucumber plants, thyme, parsley, hot and sweet peppers and an edging of santolina. A row of vines for table grapes runs along one end, an apple tree stands in one corner. It could be any family's modest vegetable garden. Its produce regularly appears on the Guérard's private table, prepared by an old-fashioned family cook who makes their meals, day in day out, in the *cuisine bourgeoise* style. Thanks to her, a delicious odour of stuffed tomatoes may float reassuringly over the park at Bachen, a guarantee that, however urbane their domain in all its parts, the Guérards continue to cherish simple country traditions.

Michel wrote in his preface to a book about south-western chefs, 'In our region, the vegetable gardens have never seemed like poor relations of their lords, the château parks. Each sings, in its own register, a hymn to the seduction of the eye or the palate; besides, I ask you, why would beds of young carrots, or fresh garlic, or the first ripe peas of June, blush to be compared with old roses, medicinal chamomile or May lilacs?' The Guérards achieve this unity of style: a suave celebration of country comforts and pleasures.

The beautiful, newly-created potager of the Ferme aux Grives.

MARC MENEAU IN SAINT-PERE-SOUS-VÉZELAY

The walled potager of Marc Meneau's restaurant L'Espérance intermingles vegetables, herbs, flowers and fruit in a complex design of parallel square beds along a central path. Each bed is divided into four triangles and somewhat raised in the centre around a tall-growing accent plant, such as angelica or a blackcurrant bush.

Meneau began as early as the late 1970s to experiment with

unusual vegetables such as parsnip chervil. He was also the first, he says, to rediscover the parsnip. Meneau hoped to provide his kitchen with vegetables and does use much of what grows here, but the bulk of what he serves today comes from small local suppliers and markets. In his potager, the vegetables are there mostly for their beauty, and for a certain educational value. He estimates that roughly sixty per cent of his customers have never seen an artichoke growing. At the same time, however, his crops also function as 'déclencheurs de recette' (springboards for recipes). And their growth helps him predict what will be ripe and ready among his suppliers as the season progresses.

ABOVE : Perfection tomato (Tomate perfection, *Vilmorin).*

*RIGHT : Garden designer Dominique Lafourcade's
plan for her garden at Les Confines,
including her potager.*

Designer visions

At the Ferme aux Grives, the potager has become purely symbolic, formally tiered around a central axis. At their country inn at La Roche Bernard in Brittany, Jacques and Solange Thorel take the stylized décor one step further still: their dining room is arranged in a classic cloister disposition, with tables set along the four roofed and glassed-in sides. In the central quadrangle, open to the air, nine small blocks of herbs and vegetables grow in a formal arrangement, with emphasis on those lasting longest and having the most architectural shapes.

Like many chefs, Thorel has a working garden elsewhere, so that this one can remain pure symbol, rich with the age-old resonances of the simple form it repeats over and over again. Professional garden designers can also be similarly bewitched by the compelling completeness of the square. Landscape architect Pascal Cribier created at Limésy in Normandy an imposing thirty-six-square courtyard esplanade, using permanent and transitory plantings: shrubs, aromatics, small fruit, perennials and vegetables, in a severe but very effective design which beautifully complements the fanciful buildings (a post-war folly). With even more daring, he imported twenty tons of earth for the garden of designer Christian Leduc on a Parisian rooftop, so that he could install a vast carpet of stonecrop (*Sedum acre*) and outline on it another magic square of ... lobelia. Within its boundaries were smaller blocks: one of lettuce and aromatics in a raised bed, another of chicory or cabbage (pale green points) grown under nine bell jars laid out, naturally, in a square. Much photographed, this latter garden no longer exists, but the former is now a classic in the genre.

Engaging the imagination and the senses, today's designer potagers remain richly sensual, keeping their feet rooted in the ground. But many also reach heavenward, into the realm of symbol and abstraction. Vegetables becomes shapes, textures, spots of colour or wisps of earthy connotation. In some cases, they disappear altogether except as echoes...

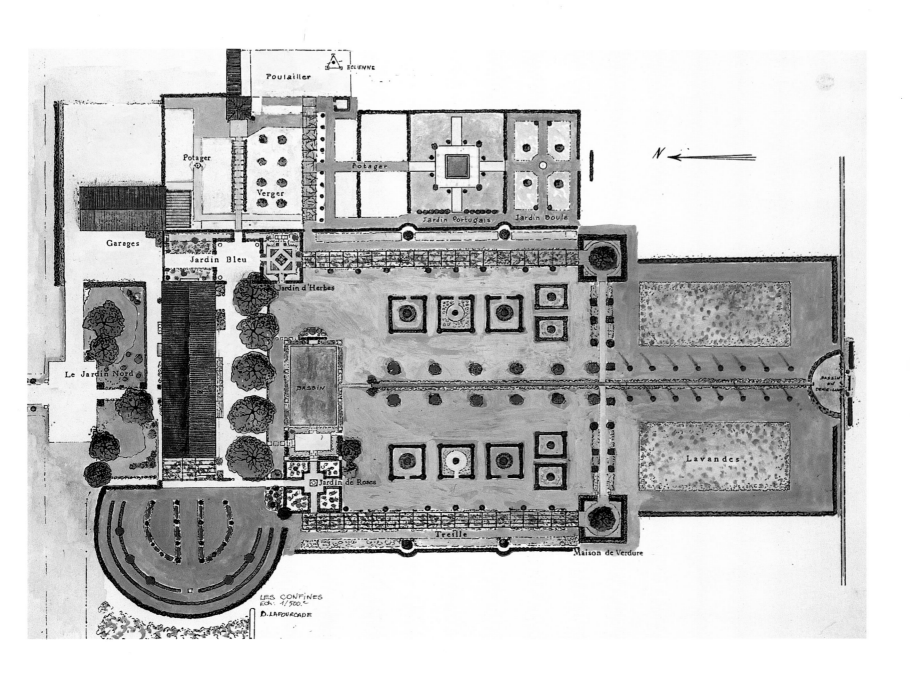

Poulailler

EOLIENNE

Potager

Potager

Verger

Jardin Portugais

Jardin Boule

Garages

Jardin Bleu

Jardin d'Herbes

N

Le Jardin Nord

BASSIN

BASSIN pour DEMIE-LUNE

Lavandes

Jardin de Roses

Treille

Maison de Verdure

LES CONFINES
Ech. 1/500.
D. LAFOURCADE

Louis Benech's cultivated fancies

ABOVE : *The orchard of the Château de Galleville occupies half the original vegetable garden, separated by a hedge. It acts now as a foil for mixed perennials and annuals, like these bright clouds of cosmos.*

RIGHT : *In keeping with château formality, these rows of vegetables are impeccably ordered, with taller vegetables and cutting flowers on one side.*

Louis Benech, one of the garden designers responsible for the restoration of the Tuileries gardens in Paris, has made an international name for himself in recent years. At first glance, he is the quintessential Parisian – a sparkling blend of charm and quick intelligence. Journalists love to interview him and inevitably depict him as an 'aesthete' with finely chiselled features and exquisite taste. Rarely does the reader glimpse a more subtle though equally Parisian characteristic: a delight in play, invention and wit.

It is quite like Louis Benech to imagine a 'make-believe' or 'false' potager – with no vegetables at all, at the Manoir de La Plesse in Normandy. He also refers to this creation somewhat nonchalantly as a *jardin de curé*, certainly not duped by the facile connotations of this phrase, but offering it as an easy way into an original conception.

The Norman manor of La Plesse, with its quaint barns and courtyard, constitutes an exceptionally fine architectural ensemble. The make-believe potager is a series of strips in the sloping lawn between the manor and its guest house. Of precisely the right size and proportions, punctuated with box balls and fruit lyres, they are planted with perennial flowers rather than vegetables. Seen from outside, they do look for all the world like a small family kitchen garden except that there is much more graduated softness in the colours, balance in their disposition, elegance in the exactness of every detail.

Below the house is a hedged flower garden. On the other side, as pendant to the potager but now linking the manor to a long barn, there will be a 'make-believe' orchard of silver-leaved pear trees, flanked by rectangles of real fruit bushes, and pergolas planted with actinidias and grapevines.

Like many Parisians, Louis Benech has country origins, both in Brittany and southern France. His parents travelled a great deal, but he had two gardening grandmothers who loved

flowers. As a child he dreamed of trees and wanted to be a forest ranger. He enjoyed visiting the Jardin des Plantes on the Ile de Ré, and the Villa Thuret gardens at Antibes. Later Benech got his garden training with plantsmen – the very best: at the Kerdalo gardens in Brittany, and with Hilliers' famous nursery, both the original English and newly created French branch. Thus he became both an expert practical plantsman and a botanist. But at the same time, his father was an architect and inspired in him a respect for form. '*Il n'a y pas de beau jardin qui ne soit construit*' (Every beautiful garden has a definite structure), he has said, and the judgment has often been quoted.

Benech started by getting a law degree in 1982 ('to do the same as everyone else'), then spent time in the merchant navy. A love of travel and discovery complements and inspires his garden explorations. Plants offer a magic opening on to the world, through the study of their origins. But this also allows the gardener to learn what conditions they need to grow best. 'The big secret', says Benech, 'is never to force nature.' By the same token, he believes that even the simplest and wildest plants have merit, depending on how they are used.

Benech travels in time as well as space, and has made a speciality of historical properties – restoring and also revitalizing their parks and gardens. He has advised the owners of two outstanding seventeenth-century Norman châteaux in this way: Galleville and Bosmelet. Both have beautiful brick and stone architecture and remnants of a formal park. Both are owned and maintained by husband-and-wife teams who devote much of their lives to the gardens. Both estates are famous above all for their elegant and imaginative potagers.

Louis Benech has become a much appreciated friend both of Monsieur and Madame Gillet at Galleville, and Monsieur and Madame de Bosmelet at the château which bears their name. It is typical of his discretion that no one can say clearly any more exactly what his contributions have been. He often drops in, he comments and advises, the owners keep lists of questions to ask on his next passage. He always leaves behind him a buzz of renewed energy. In both places, he has been responsible for very subtle and successful mixed borders edging the vegetable plots, plantings which bear witness both to his talents as a colourist and to his practical knowledge of what will grow well in different conditions. He generally makes plans ('just a sketch' says one client), advises owners (if necessary) on where to buy plants, then comes round to help set the spacing. At times, however, he digs holes himself – has even done so at the Tuileries.

In both of these châteaux's potagers, vegetable plantings occupy separate, walled sections of the larger park, and are centred on four vast rectangles. Other strips, including the elaborate mixed borders and cold frames, run along the side. In both properties, the four main sections have been organized by colour: one predominantly red, one yellow, one blue and one white. At Galleville this idea is attributed to Louis Benech. Neither household seems aware that the other has adopted a similar planting principle. In fact the results are quite different.

The Gillets have been at Galleville for some sixteen years – and the head gardener, whose wife is housekeeper, for over forty. The potager here has been restored much longer than the one at Bosmelet, and occupies only half of its original walled hectare. The rest is now given over to an exuberant orchard garden, where the fruit trees rise up from swaths of

ABOVE : The garden gate at Bosmelet opens into the lime avenue planted by Le Colinet.

LEFT : The warm brick walls at Bosmelet set off its mix of vegetables and flowers, arranged according to dominant colour.

ABOVE : Ornamental kale in the late-season ivory square. To maintain the colour coding throughout the season is a continuing challenge and hard work ... but also fun.

LEFT : Few types of gardening offer as strong a sense of the passing moment as vegetable growing. Here late afternoon sun backlights Swiss chard.

VEGETABLE GRACES   161

cleomes, Fairy roses, lavender, blue salvias, cosmos, gaura and white tobacco flowers. Benech suggested an elegant hornbeam hedge, rising to an arch in the centre, to separate orchard from potager. He proposed also a separate strip along one side of the potager for higher crops like maize, and a long row of tightly pruned fruit cordons – thus establishing a good vertical balance. His soft yellow, grey and pink mixed border extends against the far wall, a particularly harmonious composition.

Within the four main vegetable compartments at Galleville, Benech further suggested cutting away the angle of each inside corner to allow for a small square of herbs, outlined with a pebble pattern, to mark this important juncture.

At the Château de Bosmelet, the main park was laid out by Le Colinet, Le Nôtre's assistant, in 1715. Damage during World War II was terrible, and Robert de Bosmelet's mother began restoration of everything, including the potager, in the early 1950s. Using her basic designs, Laurence and Robert began improvements in 1992, first facing a mammoth pruning job on the 172 limes planted by Le Colinet. The vegetable garden opened to the public in May 1995.

Each of the four main vegetable beds, measuring about twenty-three metres square, has its own dominant colour – ruby, ivory, amber and sapphire. The red plot includes radishes, shiso (*Perilla nankensis*), red flowering salvias, dahlias and Iceland poppies, a Souvenir du Docteur Jamain rose, deep wine-coloured cornflowers, and an edging of rhubarb chard behind ornamental kale.

The white one features small button zinnias, Australian onions, white radishes, a spreading white-flowered gourd, and strawberry plants.

The blue contains ordinary cornflowers with eryngium and echinops, dwarf beans called Purple Teepee, catnip and a particularly feathery blue and purple kale.

Among the yellows, daffodils and carrots are followed by sweet peppers, Peach Melba nasturtiums and several varieties of crook-necked squash.

Each season has its peak of colour: late spring and early summer are the best moment for the ivory and ruby sections, whereas amber and sapphire are at their best in late summer and early autumn. Early spring is brightened by the proximity of the narcissus garden, where thirty-two varieties of daffodil bloom around a collection of *Magnolia stellata*.

These plantings are complemented by a lavish use of other flowers, not only annual cornflowers, poppies and salvias but dahlias, peonies and roses. The surrounding fruit trees, shrub and floral borders make a multicoloured and fragrant setting for this tapestry. Tomatoes are staked decorously along the south-facing brick wall. A stately statue of Ceres gives her blessing over all.

At Bosmelet, the gardener, who has been there over forty years, tends to shake his head over 'Madame's new ideas' – such as the introduction of purple-podded French beans. Laurence de Bosmelet, a sunny blond, is an expert flower arranger who lived in Paris until seven years ago when the family moved out to take over the domain. Her daughter, Elodie, says she knew her mother had finally adapted to country life the first time she said, 'It's raining, that will be good for the garden.'

As a pendant to the potager at Bosmelet, on the other side of the double lime avenue, Benech is now creating a spiral-shaped Discovery Garden in homage to famous botanists who brought back discoveries from all over the world. Benech has now created or advised on thirty gardens, all of which he follows closely for at least three years. He takes into consideration at the moment of creation what kind of upkeep will be available in the years to come – for example, the training and talents of professional gardeners who may be the old-fashioned kind that prunes everything to the ground! He often becomes good friends with his clients and his main weakness, he admits, is not being able to bill them. One grateful customer insisted on buying him a new car...

Benech's style is essentially painterly, though both line and colour must balance perfectly in his compositions. Within this framework, he takes delight in 'edible landscaping': herbs and vineyards at Saint-Tropez, artichokes and rhubarb chard, wine-coloured beets and blue leeks in the heart of Paris. Vegetables, like fruit and herbs, serve to enrich further his connoisseur's palate. The potager also conjures up forms – squares, the patterns of fruit cordons – as well as pleasurable agrarian connotations. But he can also imagine a pure foliage garden, another with only ten plant varieties, another with only orange and pink flowers, or another and another and another... At the same time, he exults in the suavity of perfumes. A late riser, he generally catches garden fragrance at dusk. And always there is wit: a boulder sculpted in box amuses by its presence but also adds a sumptuous and Baroque element to the garden décor.

With his provincial flower-loving grandmothers, his cosmopolitan architect father, his English training and Parisian sensibility, Louis Benech is perhaps the epitome of the Anglo-Italian gardening tradition at its best and most inventive.

RIGHT : Kohlrabi, with its delicate nuances of colour, counts among the tastiest and most beautiful of garden vegetables.

LEFT : The central rose arbour and a bright edging of Geranium psilostemon.

Gardens for the five senses:
Alain Richert

Designer Alain Richert recalls that he has only created one garden where there were no edible plants – and this was a Zen-inspired composition in Paris, made of bare earth and stone. He considers that a purely ornamental garden lacks something vital, that the traditional mixed borders are simply décors, pictures to be seen head on, or perhaps in profile, and that the pleasures of a garden should always include some sort of harvest.

Born in Morocco into a family with Swiss, Swedish, Jewish, German and Norman ancestors, Richert has always been an eccentric in the world of professional gardening. Like Benech, he began on another track entirely, in this case by studying medicine for seven years. After that he opened an art gallery in Lyons, started painting himself (encouraged by Max Ernst), took up cinema and video, made a reputation as a botanist and plant collector and finally settled into garden design, as the activity which could best satisfy all the different directions of his curiosity. Journalists describe him as a Viking with a long stride and eclectic expertise. He lives today in an old mill where his wife creates sculpture from scents and fragrances. He has published several books: on tulips, iris, and barnyard animals, as well as a guide to gardens in France. He has a gift with words, and some of his ancestors were professional storytellers.

Creator today of a number of much admired private gardens, Richert has also advised on many historical domains, including Villandry and several famous medieval cloisters. He also teaches regularly at the Ecole Nationale Supérieur du Paysage at Versailles. His work with the department of the Orne and the Ministère de l'Environnement for the enhancement of rural landscapes promises to be an example to follow, insisting as he does not on the conservation of the past in a museum sense, but on creating contemporary harmonies between a local heritage and practical, modern materials.

All of Alain Richert's gardens are multi-sensual. The one labelled as such is the celebrated Garden of the Five Senses at Yvoire, in the former potager of a splendid château jutting out over the lake of Geneva. This turreted keep provides the background for the garden enclosures which, after the court-yard Alpine garden and a cloister, are grouped in four main rectangles around a central aviary – taste, sight, smell and touch thus laid out around the birds, which represent sound. These four compartments are outlined in fruit cordons as well as hedging, but only in the space devoted to taste is every-thing edible – from the salads and red orach to the daylilies. The general design is just enough of a labyrinth to provide the pleasures of discovery from many different points of view, without frustration. The young couple who have inherited the château are devoted to this garden, fast becoming one of the most attractive provincial domains in France.

Alain Richert is not one of those designers for whom a garden must imitate nature. For him the landscape, however beautiful, is prose which a garden transforms into poetry. Perhaps the most lyrical of his gardens is the enchanted island he created at the Château de la Guyonnière, west of Poitiers.

ABOVE AND RIGHT : At Yvoire, the Garden of Colours and the Woven Garden which mixes oats (Avena sempervirens) *and the Rugosa rose Blanc Double de Coubert.*

ABOVE : The cloister fountain at Yvoire naturally attracts the ducks from the aviary.

Here the keep, built in the fourteenth century, rises on the edge of a remote rural hamlet, behind the farmyard of its latter-day dependencies, from which it is separated by a romantic drawbridge over a moat. The Dugois family have been living here since 1978, painstakingly repairing one roof after another, and devoting constant time and energy to their garden.

The moat surrounds the château, but also makes an island on the private, north-western side of the domain. Its orchard of venerable apple trees was all but overgrown with gorse and nettles when the Dugois arrived. Alain Richert came to inspect and spent a day walking around before he would even discuss plans. Both Dugois feel today that he has respected the 'soul' of the site. The word is not too strong, for the place has always had mystic connotations. The château's name may evoke a grove full of mistletoe, and this was most likely a Druid ritual spot. Tall trees enclose this magic circle even today on the far side of the moat: oaks, alders, and horse chestnut. Through this curtain, a small bridge leads to a grazing meadow beyond.

ABOVE AND OPPOSITE : In the gardens of La Guyonnière, wood appears in many forms, and on all levels.

The fairytale château – no other adjective is so apt – serves as an anchor for the island tied down by its drawbridge, but otherwise full of air and light – and birdsong.

A cascading goat willow (*Salix caprea*) stands directly across the drawbridge, rising above a wide stretch of wooden block paving planted with Corsican mint, for fragrant walking. On either side are two long rose-decked pergolas, each flanked in turn by formal, raised beds containing perennial flowers, vegetables and herbs: on the left by the Veronica Garden, on the right by the Cabbage Garden. The cabbage which gives its name to the eastern part is the highly decorative seakale or *Crambe maritima*.

Most of the floral colour here is white and blue with pale yellow accents, but there are spots of deep red peonies. Bulbs such as camassias extend the season.

At the outermost limit of this first part of the garden are two raised benches, with seats made of sweet woodruff, their rough plank backs decked with star jasmine, Dutchman's pipe (*Aristolochia elegans*) and perennial sweet pea.

The scale of plantings grows larger further away from the château, but they conceal many intimate corners. In the area behind the willow and the geometrically designed raised beds, there is an oval bee garden to the east, with medieval-style hives made of cowpats, straw and wicker, under a weathered terracotta tile roof. Honeysuckle and lemon balm outline this space, encircling rough grass in which diagonal strips of hypericum, thyme and santolina, mixed with low-growing aster, have been laid out in a pleasing pattern. Symmetrical to the bee garden to the west is a circle of small fruit bushes, with raspberries (red and yellow), and many types of black, yellow and red currants. The old apple orchard makes its presence felt on this plane, with its canopies of changing foliage, flower and fruit by season.

Further back is a formal arrangement of halesias, and a butterfly garden featuring buddleias and philadelphus, and beyond this, by the moat, a wild garden.

La Guyonnière's medieval inspiration is suggested by the use of wood as beams to outline beds, as rough fencing and as woven willow fencing; by the 'flowery mead' beneath the trees of the orchard; by the roses climbing up through branches, and by plant combinations which intermingle, for example, fennel and artichokes in among the tansy, peonies, box and

*Medieval-style hives sit at the heart of the bee garden,
surrounded by fragrant herbs.*

santolina. Its enchanted island in fact much resembles the ideal garden described by thirteenth-century writer Albertus Magnus: 'The orchard must have grass ... a veritable carpet of greenery... At its extremities will rise up trees, pears and apples ... among which vines will twine, whose foliage will protect the grass and create a welcome, cool shade... A great many aromatic and medicinal herbs will be planted, for example rue, sage and basil whose perfume will rejoice the nose, then flowers, such as violets, columbines, lilies, roses and others, which by their variety charm the eye and excite admiration... In some places the earth will be raised up to form flowery benches where one can sit and gently rest the spirit.'

As in medieval gardens, there are many levels of symbolism at La Guyonnière. The raised beds have been designed so that their proportions correspond to the average length of a tool handle, a measure Richert believes determined all practical gardening all over the world until the advent of modern technology. The very plan of the garden has a typically medieval esoteric symbolism which must remain secret to all but its owners.

The island site creates a sense of magic encirclement rather than actual enclosure. Here as at Yvoire, the viewpoints are multiple, the whole open and closed at the same time. The slight but marked differences of level on the ground create interesting patterns one feels as well as sees, and a kind of layering which gets lighter as it rises. This garden has thus a kind of transparency in spite of its intimacy. The eye can move round it like a bee seeking nectar. And so can the nose...

As for actual tasting, picking while walking round is part of the plan. But this can create problems in gardens which, like this one, are more and more visited by the general public – often here for concerts of medieval music on summer evenings.

Although some vegetables are present in the orchard, there is no potager as such at La Guyonnière. One is planned in a separate space for later on. Richert, like other designers, notes the tremendous increase in the demand for potagers by private customers but hangs back somewhat because of the problems of future upkeep. He takes on clients who will participate and not just be spectators in his creations, but must judge in each case what the realistic possibilities for future care will be.

Richert disparages the Parisian dinner-party infatuation with the *jardin de curé* or grandmother's garden, an impossible dream, he feels, mixing French formalities with peasant profusion. He does sympathize however with the nostalgia this vision reveals for a world in which a harmony existed between people, tools and the work to be done, a balance which has no doubt has disappeared for good. But he feels it is impossible to garden in tomorrow's world with the tools and techniques of yesterday.

The real interest of potagers, he suggests, gets obscured by such sentimentality. They should be appreciated rather for the unique experiences they offer, and for their special requirements: almost daily presence, for example, which allows the gardener to partake of the whole growth process from seed to crop and also to take pleasure in its repetition, over and over again. There is a ritual element in the kitchen garden. But at the same time this is ephemeral gardening, and should be enjoyed as such. Too many conventional gardeners buy perennials in pots, ready to plant, and want only those which flower non-stop, whereas it is in the nature of a flower to be a surprise, an event. Just as it is in the nature of a potager to have holes here and there due to picking. A precious sense of time and process is lost if these aspects are not cherished. Above all, the two basic parameters of the potager will always be, says Richert, the length of an arm and the width of a wheelbarrow. Their scale always remains human.

Madame Dugois paid her garden designer the ultimate compliment with respect to his work at La Guyonnière. Exclaiming modestly on its lack of grandeur with respect to the great formal French parterres, and her own inability to keep it always in prime condition, she added nonetheless that in all seasons, '*On s'y sent toujours bien*' (It is a good place to be). Whatever the predominant style of Richert's gardens (always chosen to complement the specific site), they remain places which, in the words of Albertus Magnus, 'gently rest the spirit'.

Sweet woodruff provides seats for garden benches.

The moving potager of Gilles Clément

Gilles Clément has attracted considerable attention in recent years with his conception of *le jardin en mouvement* or garden-in-flux. His creations thrive in the most varied surroundings: among them the medieval abbey of Valloires, the imposing Parc Citroën in Paris, the ambitious Riviera arboretum of the Domaine du Rayol, and the Garden of the Five Elements at Raud (see page 126). But perhaps the most famous experiment has been his own garden in the Creuse.

This little-known region, south of Tours but not yet in the Massif Central area, offers an appealing landscape of small lakes and rolling hills, partly wooded, partly cultivated. Its rural architecture of stone and lime washes in soft beiges, browns and greys unites charm and discretion, invitation and mystery. Gilles Clément was born here. He used to play in this secret valley as a child, chasing butterflies. Insects are happy here, he remarks, because there is no wind. His garden occupies a clearing in a wood of oak, grey willows (*Salix cinerea*) and hornbeam. The house he built here with his own hands sits above a stream with a rocky bed, on a steep, south-facing slope, shaded by an aged European oak (*Quercus robur*). Typically, he designed his house to fit the tree. But in 1977, even before starting work on the house, he laid out and planted his first vegetable garden.

The potager is always mentioned in accounts of his experiments, but only in passing, for it seems at first glance just the opposite of Clément's famous garden-in-flux. But Clément has never banished it, though it is not the centre of his interest. His deliberate, continuing inclusion of a potager in his evolving design tests the very limits of what a potager can be.

The garden-in-flux should not be confused with a wild garden. It is a kind of managed landscape. While it requires less work than a conventional planting (many grassy areas are mowed only once a year), it involves quite unabashed mediation of nature. A chestnut tree growing by the stream is cut back every four years to keep it in scale. Nor is there an attempt to reproduce a purely native vegetation. Admiring the chance arrival of wild evening primrose in one corner of his garden, Clément introduced next to them a group of *Gillenia trifoliata*, a delicate white-flowered plant with reddish stems, which he had admired at Sissinghurst. The picturesque rocks of the stream banks are held in place by a variety of native ferns but there is also an immense gunnera. While he cherishes his wild plants, he has not hesitated to bring in giant Himalayan lilies and Tibetan rhubarb (*Cardiocrinum giganteum*) as a way of incorporating a kind of exotic dream into the local scene. Judicious intervention on the part of the gardener is crucial to Clément's conception, but he becomes nature's partner, following her lead. Clément took his inspiration from watching the natural evolution of cleared land which, after about seven years (in a temperate climate), as it moves towards either wood or grassland, reaches the state of '*friche*'. At this stage, it contains all the elements usually found in a garden: trees, shrubs, vines, bulbs, grasses – even wild roses. He considers that to intervene and stop the progression here means creating a new

ABOVE : Nature invades in Gilles Clément's garden, but he decides where to halt it.

RIGHT : The garden-in-movement (or flux) is also made to move through, as Clément does here.

kind of garden, enriched and directed perhaps, but very much in sympathy with the natural landscape. He uses no chemicals, no artificial watering, compost rather than fertilizers. But he does prune ... hard at times. One of his most beautiful trees is a self-sown willow trimmed to show off its multiple trunks. Elsewhere clipped hornbeams stand out as smooth domes in contrast to the feathery foliage around them. In one spot where a wild smokebush spread further than he had foreseen, he has pruned the shrub so that the path uphill extends through its very centre. Another set of steps was made from railway sleepers arranged where a tree trunk had fallen and already created an indentation.

Friche – his favourite sort of terrain – usually implies abandoned land that was, at some stage, previously cultivated. Clément defines it poetically as 'an aesthetic incoherence similar to a spark, a fugitive encounter which lights up a chunk of time'.

One important and dynamic technique is to allow plants to sow themselves where they will – mulleins, columbines and buttercups are welcomed. Early in the season, mowing is restricted to creating paths through tall grass not only to preserve but even to outline and show up clumps of self-sown foxglove, giant hogweed, or mullein. As a result, the paths shift from year to year as the plants move on. Growing conditions also evolve: the removal of a dead tree will change an area from rooty shade to open sun, and the vegetation will adapt accordingly, foxglove giving way to evening primrose perhaps. Clément respects and encourages such progressions.

In most gardens, explains Clément, the plan comes first. In his conception, it is never fixed or given but develops according to the surprises nature provides – like a kind of living sculpture using natural vegetation as its medium. And Clément, like Benech and Richert, but unlike many other landscape architects, knows plants. Through them he seeks a diffuse order of being, a kind of non-linear progression, a multi-directional experience which also englobes all the senses at once. He writes that 'it is obviously difficult to imagine how such gardens will look later since their being has not been inscribed in any formal framework'. And that 'they should not be judged therefore on their form but on their aptitude to translate a certain happiness in being' ('*un certain bonheur d'exister*').

Clément delights in the creation of different atmospheres within his hidden valley: the stream bank which best represents the *jardin en mouvement*; a woodland walk enriched with rhododendrons and azaleas that passes under arches of rambling roses; a steep bank of bare rock in which miniature rockery plants have been inserted; a meadow area where a neighbour's cows come to graze. Close to the house, there is even a stretch of perennials and small shrubs managed conventionally, although all the weeding is done by hand. Machinery is kept to a minimum in this garden because Clément hates its noise. The gentle roar of the stream and birdsong add to the peaceful atmosphere rather than disturbing it.

Among all these different gardens, on the upper part of the hill, the kitchen garden remains the most formal, its nine squares surrounded on three sides by a low, clipped hornbeam hedge. Typically however, because of the potager's emplacement, the only hedges in the garden as a whole grow in its heart and not along its limits.

A potager of course is always moving – nothing evolves faster, even within one season. Yet in normal practice, nothing requires more human intervention. The nine squares have no edging to delineate them, and their paths are simply grass strips, which need regular mowing. Clément admits that he easily finds good local vegetables on local markets and he lives most of the time in Paris, when not travelling all over the world. And yet he has taken the time to design special wooden stakes for his tomato plants, looking a bit like elongated, old-

ABOVE : Clément's house, built with his own hands in this wild valley of his childhood.

LEFT : A natural rock formation allowed to evolve into a garden.

fashioned clothes pegs with rounded tops. He laments that the craftsman who carved them did not respect the proportions he was given. Thus the naturalistic garden designer continues to give considerable attention to his potager, even in its fine detailing.

Inevitably, nature's chance bounties are allowed to remain here also. Foxglove and daisies have sprung up among the beans and sorrel. Where lupins appeared, Clément added cleomes and tall white fragrant tobacco plants.

Gilles Clément's experiments might suggest those of Henry David Thoreau at Walden. There the beans gradually gave way to weeds, which Thoreau felt he had no right to remove. Clément lets some weeds remain but only those he chooses. Unlike Thoreau, he maintains his right to interfere and his potager has not succumbed over the years. And while he welcomes moles on his hillside, it is because their hills provide ideal terrain for the sowing of seeds he has collected from wild plants and which he does not scruple to sow again where and when he chooses. Clément manages the potager as he does the rest, making decisions as the need arises, in accordance with the needs of his imagination but not in thrall to any abstract philosophy or moral imperative.

Perhaps it could be said that his potager provides one atmosphere among others in the garden's varied itinerary through this hidden and verdant valley. It furnishes another modulation of Clément's carefully maintained balance between wild landscape and human intervention – a valuable variation on this theme and in that sense, an image garden. Its point is obviously not productivity. It remains rather a presence, precious for its evocation both of sensual enjoyment and of a certain, traditional rapport of man with the land. Precious also for its visual variations using hedging and squares. It has the only straight lines and right angles in the entire garden. Symbolically, the small vegetable plot communicates the designer's interest in the economies of energy and in biological flux, contributing to his meditation on time.

Rousseau would have loved Clément's garden – all in curves, full of mysterious surprises and intimate corners, self-contained, on a human scale, its artifices hidden behind a look of natural spontaneity, appealing to all the senses but also to the imagination. It is full of poetry, created by light touches. Its only view lies at the furthest point from the house, in a former quarry, where suddenly a vista opens out over Lake Chambon. The small bench suggests that this is meant to be enjoyed by a solitary *promeneur*, intent on reverie.

This garden that Clément made as his private refuge has become famous, more than any of his other creations, for its sensitive approach to nature and landscape. Here plants – vegetables among them – are not treated as objects but as players in an ever-changing biological and historical pageant.

RIGHT : Human hands sculpt here a hornbeam, there a tree trunk.

LEFT : The vegetable plot (on the right) has the only straight lines of the entire valley.

FUTURE FASHIONS

Today's potagers have undergone many metamorphoses, and more are certainly in store. Some of these may be glimpsed from year to year at the Conservatoire des Parcs et Jardins et du Paysage (Garden and Landscape Conservatory) at Chaumont-sur-Loire. Every summer, from June to September, an international competition allows young garden designers to realize temporary creations and hence be as experimental as they wish with their projects. The Island Potager (Potager en l'Ile) of 1994, designed for the Agence Européenne du Paysage, presented tin tubs of lush, exotic vegetables floating in water heated by regiments of glass bottles. Visitors were invited to man bicycle pumps to oxygenate the pool, and to squirt water on the foliage and occasionally on each other, in the summer heat, if so desired. This fanciful and ingenious conception was much admired although perhaps not much imitated by home gardeners. But there is usually at least one such original potager each year at Chaumont, and other gardens featuring 'edible landscaping'.

One major tendency today among both professionals and gifted amateurs is to make the potager one variation on the garden's theme, or one stop on an itinerary – as in the garden of Gilles Clément. In such compositions, vegetables may be concentrated into one semi-formal space, but they also spill out of the potager into other sections – salads and rhubarb in the flower borders, for example. South of Mont-Saint-Michel, for example, retired nurseryman Jean Renault has created a park on about five hectares, Les Renaudies, in which a vast ornamental potager is one stop along the path which moves among some two hundred varieties of hydrangea and 150 types of ornamental cherry. Rather more intimate is the Château de Momas near Pau, where Marie-Josèphe Teillard perpetuates a highly refined version of the *jardin de grand'-mère*, which if she were English would be described as a cottage garden. One stop on the itinerary round her thriving collections is a picturesque potager with many unusual types of perpetual onion and leek, a plant she calls 'strawberry spinach' (*Chenopodium capitatum*) with edible leaves and red berries, an oenothera nicknamed 'poor man's ham', Armenian cucumbers, Mexican and Peruvian physalis, perennial cabbage, and, in her greenhouse, lychees and pink bananas. She loves to explain and advise on the use of these rarities, pointing out for example that chayotes should be picked only when 'their tongues stick out'.

ABOVE : Detail of the Island Potager at the Chaumont Conservatoire.

LEFT : Apple cordons flank the path in the kitchen garden designed by Dominique Lafourcade.

In a private garden near Paris designed by Jean-Pierre Bénet and Thierry Chastagnier, each square vegetable bed has a corner of flowers set off by a wooden screen and marked by a white standard rose (Iceberg and Queen of the Musk).

North of Paris, near Senlis, are the elaborate gardens of La Verderonne. Abandoned for a hundred years, they now spread around the former stables and outhouses of the Château de Verderonne. Here, since 1974, Dr Henri Cassoly and his friends, Marie and Guillaume de Panafieu, have divided the domain between them. Together they have developed a delightful sequence of gardens which now serve as the setting for chamber music and theatricals, art and craft exhibitions and garden salons. Here too the itinerary is varied and full of surprises, starting from a high towered dovecote surrounded by old roses and moving past a rare *pédiluve* or sloping pool for bathing horses, draped with a sumptuous wisteria. There follows an elegant nineteenth-century greenhouse presiding in a semi-formal garden echoing the *jardin de curé* vision; then a water garden stretching by the old milking sheds and a smooth lake mirroring tall trees. There are many sophisticated blends of foliage texture and colour as well as flowers, which start blooming with the hellebores and jonquils of early spring and continue through to the dahlias and asters of autumn. Varied textures of brick and stone enhance the garden's own diversity, which includes extensive collections of roses and clematis. Dr Cassoly's residence, called the Maison aux Hirondelles, contains an old well, a bread oven and a cheese-making pantry.

'Edible landscaping' is a principle that is constantly adhered to here: the aromatic purple-blue annual borage grows all over the garden – particularly effectively when planted next to the colourful (though poisonous) horticultural spurge *Euphorbia griffithii* 'Fireglow' and the wild yellow asphodel. Wild iris are mixed with red orach and white-purply clary sage. Ornamental garlics, perennial celery, self-sowers like poppies, scabious and salad burnet pop up all over the place. The potager proper emerges as one element among many, stripes behind a low box hedge pruned in wavy patterns. These display sorrel, salads, poppies, strawberries, violets, parsley, onions, chicory allowed to flower with its electric blue blossoms, feverfew, roquette, a few tomato plants and a triangle of roses round a hazelnut bush – informal mixtures with country connotations.

This is a garden of considerable refinement. It is a good example of the current genre. Neither château potager nor genuine *jardin de curé*, not predominantly a collector's nor yet a designer's domain, but a mixture of all these ingredients at once in a harmonious, personal blend.

Many more examples could be cited from all over the country. The fashion does have its excesses of course – some creations recall a Disney fantasy. Among the worthwhile efforts, however, some seduce by the pure geometries of fruit forms and vegetable squares, others by their sensuality, or their suggestion of well-ordered family economy – which adds the satisfaction of good conscience to more palpable pleasures.

But the current proliferation of potagers, in France as elsewhere, is no mere fad. It is part of a more general move away from the garden experienced only as picture or spectacle, predominantly visual, towards a conception at one and the same time more dynamic and more multi-sensual. Simple décor, however elegant, is no longer enough. Potagers have deeper roots...

Today's potagers also reveal that some ancient gaps are being bridged: for example, between utilitarian and ornamental gardening – not only (as it always was) in the farm garden but now even for the most avant-garde designers. And the kitchen garden experience, as seen earlier, also helps establish new connections between city and country.

The gardening press keeps the public informed about and excited by ongoing trends, some specializing in designer visions, others recounting social experimentation. Are the dreams they promote simply escapist, or do they lead to real changes? Historian Jean-Paul Pigeat suggests that, for pessimists, the photographs of glossy magazines invite us to enjoy natural rhythms vicariously, without actually experiencing smells and dirt. But the optimist, he says, will argue that today's gardening fashions are helping us learn to respect the world's natural balances.

However far-reaching its influence may eventually prove, the French potager is already inspiring a new creativity which touches, more than any other kind of gardening, people from all backgrounds and all corners of the country.

A 'tour de France' of French herb and vegetable gardens

The following are potagers I visited in preparing this book, but many more beautiful examples can be discovered all over France. These suggestions are presented in categories broadly corresponding to the themes of the book. Thus the same address may appear in several places – a clue to a garden that is even more worth visiting! As opening hours and conditions vary, telephone for up-to-date information before going.

Château potagers

Bellecoste, Château de. Caissargues, 30230 Bouillargues (near Nîmes). Owner: Madame Jeanne-Marie du Tremblay. Tel. (4) 66 20 18 26. Mixed potager and extensive iris collection, good plant fair early May.

Berzé le Châtel, Château de. 71960 Pierreclos (Burgundy, near Macon). Owners: Comte and Comtesse de Thy de Milly. Tel. (3) 85 36 60 83. Terraced garden. Sale of wine on the property.

Bosmelet, Château de. 76720 Auffay (Upper Normandy). Owners: Monsieur and Madame Robert de Bosmelet. Tel. (2) 35 32 81 07. Fax (2) 35 32 84 62. Elegant seventeenth-century domain with 'rainbow' potager and rare vegetables.

Bourdaisière, Château de la. 37270 Montlouis (Loire valley, east of Tours). Owner: Prince de Broglie. Tel. (2) 47 45 16 31. Fax (2) 47 45 09 11. Potager being designed by Madame de Saint-Venant of Valmer.

Bournel, Château de. 25680 Cubry (Jura, eastern France). Owner: Monsieur Lionel de Moutiers. Tel. (3) 81 86 00 10. Fax (3) 81 86 01 06. Late nineteenth-century park, orchards.

Chaize, Château de la. Odenas, 69460 Saint-Etienne-des-Oullières (Beaujolais region). Owner: Madame Roussy de Sales. Tel. (4) 74 03 40 26 or (4) 74 03 41 05. Sale of wine on the property. Garden only open on special national visiting days in June. One of the most beautiful.

Closel, Domaine de. Place du Mail, Savennières 41170 Saint-Georges-sur-Loire (near Angers). Owners: Monsieur and Madame Bazin de Jessey. Tel. (2) 41 72 81 00. Sale of wine on the property. Garden only open on national visiting days in June. Edging the Loire, old-fashioned family style.

Dauphin, Château. 63230 Pontgibaud (Auvergne, west of Clermont-Ferrand.). Owners: Monsieur and Madame Gabriel de Germiny. Tel. (4) 73 88 73 39. Fax (4) 73 88 92 42. Beautiful interiors, sunken potagers praised by Montaigne in the sixteenth century.

Fey, Château de. 89300 Villecien (Yonne). Tel. (3) 86 63 18 34. Fax (3) 86 63 01 33. Owner: Anne Willan, celebrated chef and writer of cookery books. Her potager is at the cooking school at the château. In the US: La Varenne at the Greenbrier, White Sulphur Springs, WV 24986. Tel. (800) 624 6070 or (304) 536 1110. Fax (304) 536 7919.

Galleville, Château de. 76560 Doudeville (Upper Normandy). Ambassador and Mrs Robert Gillet. Tel. (2) 35 96 54 65. Elegant domain combining the seventeenth century with contemporary design. Potager designed by Louis Benech.

Grènerie, Château de. 19510 Salon-la-Tour (Corrèze). Owners: Monsieur and Madame Charpentier. Tel. (5) 55 73 40 25. Formal château gardens.

Guyonnière, Château de la. 79420 Beaulieu-sous-Parthenay (west of Poitiers). Owner: Madame Valérianne Dugois. Tel. (5) 49 64 22 99. Fax (5) 49 64 06 20. An island orchard garden designed by Alain Richert, near a turreted château. Concerts in summer.

La Massonnière. 72540 Saint-Christophe-en-Champagne (Sarthe). Owner: Monsieur Joël Moulin. Tel. (2) 43 88 61 26. Elegant manor-house garden, walled potager, topiary. Open weekends. A particularly beautiful and well-maintained example.

Malouinière du Bos. Quelmer, 35400 Saint-Malo (Brittany). Owners: Monsieur and Madame René Picard. Tel. (2) 99 81 40 11. Fax (2) 99 31 42 16. Wonderful wild site, eighteenth-century architecture.

Miromesnil, Château de. 76550 Tourville-sur-Arques (Upper Normandy, 8 km south of Dieppe). Owner: Monsieur de Vogüé. Tel. and Fax (2) 35 85 02 80.

Seventeenth to nineteenth centuries, one of the most picturesque and best-known.

Momas, Château de. 64230 Lescar (north of Pau in the Pyrenees). Owner: Madame Marie-Josèphe Teillard. Tel. (5) 59 77 14 71. Manor-house garden with many collectors' items, rare vegetables, plant fair in September.

Mongenan, Château de. 16 rue Mongenan, 33640 Portets (east of Bordeaux). Owner: Madame Florence Mothe. Tel. (5) 56 67 18 11. Fax (5) 56 67 08 11. Exuberant walled garden inspired by Jean-Jacques Rousseau who was a friend of the eighteenth-century owner. Rare plants, much seasonal colour.

Opme, Château d'. 63540 Romagnat (Auvergne, south of Clermont-Ferrand). Owners: Monsieur and Madame Philippe Durin. Tel. (4) 73 87 54 85. Elegant terraced potager.

Pêcheurs, Château des. 45230 La Bussière (between the Loire and Burgundy). Owner: Madame de Chasseval. Tel. (2) 38 35 93 35. Fax (2) 38 35 94 13. Fairytale moated castle housing a fishing museum, seventeenth-century to contemporary gardens.

Potager du Roi. 4, rue Hardy, 78000 Versailles. Houses the Ecole Nationale Supérieur d'Horticulture and the Ecole Nationale Supérieure du Paysage. Tel. (1) 39 50 60 87. Famous seventeenth-century creation variously restored and kept up since.

Saint-Jean-de-Beauregard, Château de. 91940 Saint-Jean-de-Beauregard (23 km south-west of Paris). Owners: Monsieur and Madame de Curel. Tel. (1) 60 12 00 01. Fax (1) 60 12 56 31. Celebrated plant fairs held here in April for perennials and in November for vegetables.

Sayette, Château de la. 79340 Vasles (30 km west of Poitiers). Owners: Monsieur and Madame Emmanuel de la Sayette. Tel. (5) 49 69 94 93. Recent restoration of seventeeth- and eighteenth-century garden of much charm.

Saint-Paterne, Château de. 72610 Saint-Paterne (Normandy, near Alençon). Owner: Monsieur Charles-Henri de Valbray. Tel. (2) 33 27 54 71. Fax (2) 33 29 16 71. Nineteenth-century park with colourful Asian immigrant potager in one corner.

Elegant 'chambres d'hôte' – bed and breakfast with optional dinner.

Théret, Château du. 23000 La Saunière (south of the Loire valley). Owner: Monsieur Alain de Reynal de Saint-Michel. Tel. (5) 55 80 01 35. Picturesque, recently restored potager.

Tournelay, Château de. 79250 Neuil-sur-Argent (west of Poitiers). Owners: Monsieur and Madame de Lassus. Tel. (5) 49 65 61 13. Large colourful walled garden with period greenhouses.

Valmer, Jardins de. 37210 Chançay (Loire valley, just east of Tours). Owner: Madame Alix de Saint-Venant. Tel. (2) 47 52 93 12. Fax (2) 47 52 26 92. Superb formal terraced château gardens with vegetables on the lowest level.

Vayres, Chateau de. 33870 Vayres (near Bordeaux). Owner: Monsieur Etrillard. Tel. (5) 57 74 85 15. Fax (5) 57 84 92 00. Formal château gardens, potager and delightful aromatic garden.

Villandry, Château de. 37510 Villandry (Loire valley). Owner: Monsieur Henri Carvallo. Tel. (2) 47 50 02 09. The most famous of French ornamental potagers, unique and wonderful, though too formal to provide a model for current taste.

Jardins de curé (variations on the theme according to various definitions of the genre)

Brihat, Monsieur Denis. Les Blayons, 84480 Bonnieux (Provence, between Aix and Avignon). Tel. (4) 90 75 81 85. Fax (4) 90 75 99 87. The owner, a talented artist, sells from home his haunting and beautiful photographs, mostly of vegetables from his garden. Charming seventeenth-century family home in the heart of an industrial landscape, but worth the detour.

Clos du Coudray. Hameau du Coudray, 76850 Etaimpuis (Upper Normandy). Owner: Monsieur Jean Le Bret. Tel. (1) 34 34 96 85. Herb garden and mixed borders, plant collections, created by one of the leading French horticultural journalists.

Jardin des Renaudies. Les Meserais, 53120 Colombiers-du-Plessis (east of Mont-Saint-Michel). Owner: Monsieur Jean Renault. Tel. (2) 43 08 02 08.

Fax (2) 43 08 69 83. A five hectare park with many different collections and gardens, including an intimate floral potager, all created by a dedicated retired nurseryman. Ecomuseum.

Maison des Champs de Pierre Corneille. 502 rue Pierre Corneille, 76650 Petit-Couronne (south-western suburb of Rouen). Owner: Département de la Seine-Maritime. Curator: Evelyne Poirel. Tel. (2) 35 68 13 89. Fax (2) 35 70 25 16. Charming country home of seventeenth-century French playwright.

Momas, Château de. 64230 Lescar (north of Pau in the Pyrenees). Owner: Madame Marie-Josèphe Teillard. Tel. (5) 59 77 14 71. Manor-house garden with many collectors' items, rare vegetables, plant fair in September.

Mongenan, Château de. 16 rue Mongenan, 33640 Portets (east of Bordeaux). Owner: Madame Florence Mothe. Tel. (5) 56 67 18 11. Fax (5) 56 67 08 11. Exuberant walled garden inspired by Jean-Jacques Rousseau who was a friend of the eighteenth-century owner. Rare plants, much seasonal colour.

Musée Départemental du Prieuré (former home of painter Maurice Denis). 2bis, rue Maurice Denis, 78100 Saint-Germain-en-Laye (west of Paris). Owner: the Département des Yvelines. Tel. (1) 39 73 77 87. Fax (1) 39 73 75 29. Romantic potager and orchard at the bottom of the garden.

Pigeard, Claude. Rue de la Mairie, 95420 Wy-dit-Joli-Village (near Mantes-la-Jolie, west of Paris). Tel. (1) 34 67 41 79. Besides the beautiful vicarage garden with its old roses, potager and herb garden, there are Roman baths and fascinating collections of tools and crafts.

Les Prés d'Eugénie (restaurant-hotel Relais-Châteaux). 40320 Eugénie-les-Bains (south-east of Bordeaux). Owners: Christine and Michel Guérard. Tel. (5) 58 51 19 50. Fax (5) 58 51 10 10. Old-fashioned herb and rose garden (*jardin de curé*) and stylized potager by the Ferme aux Grives (the Guérards' bistro).

Verderonne, Château de la. 7bis and 9 rue du Château, 60140 Verderonne (Picardy, between Paris and Amiens). Owners: Dr Henry Cassoly and Monsieur and Madame de Panafieu. Tel. (3) 44 73 10 67. Imaginative blend of edible and ornamental gardening in the grounds of a château, around stables and lake.

Designer gardens

Bastide de Moustiers. La Grisolière, 04360 Moustiers-Sainte-Marie. Tel. (2) 92 70 47 48. Fax (2) 92 70 47 48. Owner: Alain Ducasse, celebrated chef of Monaco and Paris. Elegant ornamental potager designed by Riviera architect Jean Mus (Rue Frédéric Mistral, 06530 Cabris. Tel. (4) 93 60 54 50. Fax (4) 93 60 52 81) and planted by vegetable expert Jean-Luc Danneyrolles (see 'Heirloom Vegetables' below).

Bosmelet, Château de. 76720 Auffay (Upper Normandy). Owners: Monsieur and Madame Robert de Bosmelet. Tel. (2) 35 32 81 07. Fax (2) 35 32 84 62. Elegant seventeenth-century domain with contemporary creations, some by Louis Benech.

'La Coquetterie'. Limésy, 76570 Pavilly (Upper Normandy). Tel. (2) 35 91 28 01. Owner: Madame de Bagneux. Designed by Pascal Cribier.

Conservatoire International des Parcs et Jardins et du Paysage. Ferme du Château de Chaumont, 41150 Chaumont-sur-Loire. Tel. (2) 54 20 99 22. Fax (2) 54 20 99 24. Experimental plots with shows all summer by garden designers selected from competitors all over the world, changing yearly. There is almost always a potager among them.

Domaine de Raud. BP 20, 38710 Mens, Isère. Tel. (4) 76 34 80 80. Fax (4) 76 34 84 02. Centre Terre Vivante: experimental centre for ecologically sound living with several trial vegetable gardens. Parts laid out by Gilles Clément.

Galleville, Château de. 76560 Doudeville (Upper Normandy). Ambassador and Mrs Robert Gillet. Tel. (2) 35 96 54 65. Elegant domain combining the seventeenth century with contemporary design. Potager designed by Louis Benech.

Guyonnière, Château de la. 79420 Beaulieu-sous-Parthenay (west of Poitiers). Owner: Madame Valérianne Dugois. Tel. (5) 49 64 22 99. Fax (5) 49 64 06 20. An island orchard garden designed by Alain Richert, near a turreted château. Concerts in summer.

Yvoire, Château d'. Rue du Lac, 74140 Yvoire (near Geneva). Tel. (4) 50 72 88 80. Fax (4) 50 72 90 80. Owners: Monsieur and Madame d'Yvoire. The Garden of the Five Senses: contemporary gardens of medieval inspiration on the theme of the five senses designed by Alain Richert.

Gardens of medieval inspiration (other than châteaux)

Domaine Médiéval des Champs. Le Villard, 48230 Chanac (Lozère, central France). Curator: Madame Anne Trémolet de Villers. Tel. (4) 66 48 25 00. A wonderful medieval farmstead with animals, crafts, imposing architecture and a working potager.

Ecomusée d'Ungersheim. BP 71, 68190 Ungersheim (Alsace, near Mulhouse). Tel. (3) 89 74 44 74. Fax (3) 89 48 15 30. Fascinating re-creation of local styles with many country kitchen gardens including one with vegetables grown in the sixth century.

Limeuil, Jardin-Musée de. 24510 Limeuil (Dordogne). Owners: Michel and Véronique Guignard. Tel. (5) 53 63 32 06. Fascinating re-creation of typical gardens from neolithic to modern (Lascaux is nearby).

Musée de l'Oeuvre Notre-Dame. 3, place du Château, 67000 Strasbourg. Tel. (3) 88 52 50 00. In the courtyard of the cathedral museum of Strasbourg, very picturesque, surrounded by high Gothic houses.

Prieuré de Notre Dame d'Orsan. 18170 Maisonnais. Tel. (2) 48 56 27 50. Situated 50 km south of Bourges, a splendid and imaginative re-creation. Open in the summer.

Prieuré de Saint-Cosme. 37520 La Riche (western suburb of Tours). Tel. (2) 47 37 32 70. Former dwelling of Renaissance poet Pierre de Ronsard, a charming restoration but most of the roses are modern.

Prieuré Saint-Michel. 61120 Crouttes (Lower Normandy). Owners: Monsieur and Madame Chahine. Tel. (2) 33 39 15 15. Fax (2) 33 36 15 16. An agreeable mix of period and contemporary creation.

Prieuré de Salagon. 04300 Mane (Alps of Provence). Owner: Conseil Général des Alpes de Haute Provence. Tel. (4) 92 75 31 25. Beautiful Romanesque abbey buildings surrounded by gardens, including medieval potager re-creation and herb parterre.

Chefs' kitchen gardens (all are restaurants and hotels)

Bardet: Jean Bardet, 57 rue Groison, 37000 Tours. Owners: Jean and Sophie Bardet. Chef: Jean Bardet. Tel. (2) 47 41 41 11. Fax (2) 47 51 68 72. Famous cook and gastronome but also collector of rare vegetables.

Charial: Oustau de Baumanière, 13520 Maussane. Tel. (4) 90 54 33 07. Fax (4) 90 54 40 46. Owner and chef: Jean-André Charial. The vegetable gardens of Baumanière are not open to the public but there are elegant formal herb gardens at the Cabro d'Oro, the sister restaurant.

Chibois: La Bastide de Saint-Antoine, Avenue Henri Dunant, Quartier Saint-Antoine, 06300 Grasse. Tel. (4) 93 38 70 72. Fax (4) 93 42 03 42. Owner and chef: Jacques Chibois. Elegant eighteenth-century domain where the original potager site and cold frames still exist, among wonderful olive orchards. Plans are afoot to restore and make good use of the kitchen garden for the table.

Ducasse: La Bastide de Moustiers, La Grisolière, 04360 Moustiers-Sainte-Marie (Alpes-de-Haute-Provence). Tel. (4) 92 70 47 48. Fax (4) 92 70 47 48. Owner: Alain Ducasse, celebrated chef of Monaco and Paris. Elegant ornamental potager designed by Riviera architect Jean Mus and planted by vegetable expert Jean-Luc Danneyrolles.

Gleize: La Bonne Etape, Château-Arnoux, 04160 (Alpes-de-Haute-Provence). Owner and chef: Jany Gleize. Tel. (4) 92 64 00 09. Fax (4) 92 64 37 36. Family-style inn with herbs and vegetables for its celebrated table. A great classic.

Guérard: Les Prés d'Eugénie (Relais-Châteaux), 40320 Eugénie-les-Bains (south-east of Bordeaux). Owners: Christine and Michel Guérard. Tel. (5) 58 51 19 50. Fax (5) 58 51 10 10. Old-fashioned herb and rose garden (*le jardin de curé*) and stylized potager by the Ferme aux Grives (the Guérards' bistro).

Husser: Le Cerf, 30 rue de Général-de-Gaulle, 67520 Marlenheim (Alsace, east of Strasbourg, near Saverne). Owners: Robert and Michel Husser and their families. Tel. (3) 88 87 73 73. Fax (3) 88 87 68 08. Family inn with traditional appeal and contemporary verve, thanks

to two generations of chefs. The potager is elsewhere, visible only on request if the chef is not too busy.

Marcon: Auberge des Cimes, 43290 Saint-Bonnet-le-Froid (west of Rhône valley). Owner and chef: Régis Marcon. Tel. (4) 71 59 93 72. Fax (4) 71 59 93 40. A two-star chef in a country inn, specializing in rare vegetables. Herb garden.

Meneau: L'Espérance, 89450 Saint-Père-sous-Vézelay (Burgundy). Owner and chef: Marc Meneau. Tel. (3) 86 33 20 45. Fax (3) 86 33 26 15. Intimate and exuberant potager laid out in squares.

Sammut: Auberge la Fenière, Route de Cadenet, 84160 Cadenet. Owner and chef: Reine Sammut. Tel. (4) 90 68 11 79. Fax (4) 90 68 18 60.

Thorel: Auberge Bretonne, 2, place Du Guesclin, 56130 La Roche-Bernard (southern coast of Brittany). Owners and chef: Jacques and Solange Thorel. Tel. (2) 99 90 60 28. Fax (2) 99 90 85 00. Family inn with elegant courtyard show potager. Produce from the chef's farm outside the town.

Willan: Anne Willan, celebrated chef and writer of cookery books. Her potager is at the cooking school of La Varenne at the Château de Fey, 89300 Villecien, Tel. (3) 86 63 18 34. Fax (3) 86 63 01 33. In the US: La Varenne at the Greenbrier, White Sulphur Springs, WV 24986. Tel. (800) 624 6070 or (304) 536 1110. Fax (304) 536 7919.

Two chefs without gardens, but who gave advice on vegetables for this book

Daguin: André Daguin. Hôtel de France, Place de la Libération, 32000 Auch (south-west France). Tel. (5) 62 05 00 44. Fax (5) 62 05 88 44. Although specializing in poultry and foie gras, a great expert on how vegetables are grown and used in a part of France where maize and dried beans are part of the traditional diet.

Taffarello: Claude Taffarello. Auberge du Poids Public, 31540 Saint Félix-Lauragais (south-west France). Tel. (5) 61 83 00 20. Fax (5) 61 83 86 21. Interesting contemporary treatment of rich local resources.

Community, allotment or 'family' gardens (not always open for public walks, check before going)

Cajarc. 46160 Cajarc. Public walk along the banks of the Lot, called Le Faubourg.

Fontainebleau, Association des Jardins Ouvriers. President: Maurice Cuvelier, 48 rue d'Avon, 77300 Fontainebleau. Tel. (1) 64 22 17 26. Several sites around the town, colourful and lively.

Hortillonnages, Les. In Picardy, north of Paris. Association pour la Protection et la Sauvegarde du Site de l'Environnement des Hortillonnages. President: Monsieur Nisso Pélossof, 54 boulevard Beauvillé, 80000 Amiens. Tel. (3) 22 92 12 18. Unique water gardens, classified by UNESCO.

Ivry, Jardins Familiaux d'. Suburb of Paris. Association President: Dr Jacques Perreau, 118 avenue Danielle Casanova, 94200 Ivry. Tel. (1) 46 58 59 96. Among the most famous, but private except on special visit days.

Saint-Paterne, Château de. 72610 Saint-Paterne. Owner: Charles-Henri de Valbray. Tel. (2) 33 27 54 71. Fax (2) 33 29 16 71. Community of Asian gardeners.

Tours. Several allotment associations, especially the picturesque gardens of the former hospital of Les Minimes. For information about visits, contact the town hall of the La Riche suburb: Mairie de la Riche, place du Maréchal Leclerc, 37520 La Riche. Tel. (2) 47 37 33 95. Fax (2) 47 38 11 52.

Tulle. Corrèze. Allotment association. President: Monsieur Chabrillangeas, 17D rue Dr Valette, 19000 Tulle. Tel. (5) 55 26 71 54. Several beautiful sites in a small city in the heart of France, managed by an energetic association.

Villejuif. Parc Départemental des Hautes-Bruyères, avenue de la République, 94800 Villejuif. 8 kilometres from Paris. Contact the town hall. Tel. (1) 43 99 82 80. Butterfly shelters designed by architect Renzo Piano.

and also:

Ligue Française du Coin de la Terre et du Foyer, 11 rue Desprez, 75014 Paris. Tel. (1) 45 40 40 45 or (1) 45 40 68 90. Fax (1) 45 40 78 90. Philippe Pierson, general delegate.

Musée des Maraîchers, 9 chemin du Mont Giffard, 95160 Montmorency, Tel. (1) 34 17 25 63. Market gardens of Paris museum.

Heirloom vegetables

A mixture of sources, some offering rare seeds by mail, others visits to experimental gardens, many giving workshops, one a small cannery, but all engaged in preserving precious old varieties.

'Le Potager d'un curieux', Jean-Luc Danneyrolles. 'La Molière', Saignon, 84400 Apt. Rare vegetables available on the Saturday morning market in Apt, rue de la Sous-Préfecture. Sale of seeds and seedlings by mail.

Centre Terre Vivante, Domaine de Raud, BP 20, 38711 Mens, Isère. Tel. (4) 76 34 80 80. Fax (4) 76 34 84 02. Many workshops and exhibits and several experimental vegetable gardens, in a very beautiful setting.

Chaudière, Maurice. L'Atelier Maladroit, La Sarrazine, 07460 Berrias. Tel. (4) 75 39 31 74 or (4) 75 39 00 19. An expert in grafting – aubergine on tobacco roots, for example. Workshops, visits, apiculture and solar cooking.

Couplan, François. Author and director of the Institut de Recherches sur les Propriétés de la Flore (Research Institute on the Properties of Flora), Haut Ougreas, 04330 Barrême. Tel. (4) 92 34 25 29 or (4) 92 34 27 65. Research and experimentation on unusual vegetables. Summer séminars on wild edible plants, with emphasis on gastronomy.

Ferme de Sainte Marthe, Philippe Desbrosses. BP 10, 41700 Cour-Cheverny (Loire valley). Experimental garden and very full seed catalogue.

Ferme-Parc: Oh! Légumes Oubliés, Domaine de Belloc, 33670 Sadirac. Tel. (5) 56 30 61 00. Fax (5) 56 30 60 30. Director Bernard Lafon. Old-fashioned canning factory for rare vegetables with a show garden and tastings. Home of the association Les Amis d'Archimboldo.

Harvey, Francois and Simone. Combe Basse, 30460 Lasalle. Connoisseur and producer, he sells produce on Friday mornings at the market of Saint-Jean-du-Gard. Sells seeds by correspondence.

Jardin des Renaudies. Les Meserais, 53120 Colombiers-du-Plessis (east of Mont-Saint-Michel). Owner: Mr Jean Renault. Tel. (2) 43 08 02 08. Fax (2) 43 08 69 83. A five-hectare park with many different collections and gardens, including an intimate floral potager, all created by a dedicated retired nurseryman. Ecomuseum.

Jean Bardet (restaurant). 57 rue Groison, 37000 Tours. Owners: Jean and Sophie Bardet. Chef: Jean Bardet. Tel. (2) 47 41 41 11. Fax (2) 47 51 68 72. Famous gastronome but also collector of rare vegetables.

Momas, Château de. Madame Marie-Josèphe Teillard. Château de Momas, 64230 Lescar.Tel. (5) 59 77 14 71. Very interesting selection of old vegetable varieties and new discoveries. Plant fair.

Terre de Semences. Jardin botanique de la Mhotte. Director Dominique Guillet, Chante-Alouette, 03210 Saint Menoux. Tel. (4) 70 43 96 92. Fax (4) 70 43 96 83. Well-stocked seed catalogue, specialists in amaranths.

Bibliography

Adams, William Howard. *The French Garden 1500–1800*. London, 1979.

Beauthéac, Nadine (ed.). *Les Jardins du retour, les carnets de l'exotisme*. Poitiers, 1994.

Bergues, Martine. 'Jardins de savoirs et jardins miroirs' in *Quercy Recherche* no. 82, Sept.–Dec. 1995.

Beuchert, Patricia and Collaert, Jean-Paul. *Le Beau jardin du paresseux*. Paris, 1986.

Bonnel, Rolant G. *Jardins et châteaux*, Dalhousie French Studies special issue, Vol. 29, Halifax, 1994.

Bosco, Henri. *Le Trestoulas*. Paris, 1935.

Bronzert, Kathleen and Sherwin, Bruce (eds). *The Glory of the Garden*. New York, 1993.

Cabedoce, Béatrice. *Cent ans d'histoire des jardins ouvriers 1896–1996*. Paris, 1996.

Carvallo, Robert. *Joachim Carvallo et Villandry*. n.p., 1990.

Charlton, D.G. *New Images of the Natural in France*. Cambridge, 1985.

Colette. *La Naissance du Jour*. Paris, 1969.

——— *Prisons et paradis*. Paris, 1986.

——— *Sido*. Paris, 1901.

Couplan, François. *Retrouvez les légumes oubliés*. Paris, 1986.

Defay, Bruno. *Trésors de courges et de potirons*. Paris, n.d.

Delaporte, Jacqueline. *La Maison des champs de Pierre Corneille*. Rouen, 1984.

Erkmann-Chatrian. *Gens d'Alsace et de Lorraine*. Paris, 1993.

Ford, Ford Madox. *Provence*. London, 1962.

Fortescue, Winifred. *Perfume from Provence*. Edinburgh, 1950.

Gascar, Pierre. *Un jardin de curé*. Paris, 1979.

Giono, Jean. *Provence*. Paris, 1993.

Givry, Jacques de and Perillon, Yves. *Versailles: Le Potager du Roi*. Les Loges-en-Josas, 1993.

Goldin, Frederick. *Lyrics of the Troubadours and Trouvères*. New York, 1973.

Goodey, Jack. *The Culture of Flowers*. Cambridge, 1993.

Gouvion, Colette and Huclie, Marielle. *Le Roman du potager*. Rodez, 1994.

Grimal, Pierre. *L'Art des jardins*. Paris, 1974.

Gromort, George. *L'Art des jardins*. Paris, n.d.

Hunt, John Dixon (ed.). *The Pastoral Landscape*. Hanover, London and Washington DC, 1992.

James, Henry. *A Little Tour in France*. Oxford, 1984.

Le Jardin astucieux des Quatre Saisons, Terre Vivante. Paris, 1992.

'Spécial Cinquante' in *Le Jardin du cheminot* no. 276, July–Aug. 1993.

Jellicoe, Geoffrey and Susan, Goode, Patrick and Lancaster, Michael (eds). *The Oxford Companion to Gardens*. Oxford, 1986.

Lassus, Bernard (ed.). *Hypothèses pour une troisième nature*. London and Paris, 1992.

Le Dantec, Denise and Jean-Pierre. *Le Roman des jardins de France: leur histoire*. Paris, 1985.

——— *Reading the French Garden: Story and History*. Cambridge, Mass., 1990.

Le Sauvage. 'Le jardin: modèle de gestion du monde' in *Le Nouvel Observateur* no. 71, Summer 1980.

Lequenne, Fernand. *Olivier de Serres: agronome et soldat de Dieu*. Paris, 1983.

Lieutaghi, Pierre. *Jardin des savoirs, jardin d'histoire*. Mane: Les Alpes de Lumière 110-11, n.d.

Lloyd, Christopher. *In My Garden*. London, 1993.

Moray, Paul. *Ecoverger: un verger de nature frugale*. Montpellier, 1990.

Mosser, Monique and Nys, Philippe (eds). *Le Jardin, art et lieu de mémoire*. Vassivière-en-Limousin, 1995.

Mosser, Monique and Teyssot, Georges (eds). *The History of Garden Design*. London and Cambridge, Mass., 1991.

Mothe, Florence. *Toutes hontes bues: un siècle de vin et de négoce à Bordeaux*. Paris, 1992.

Mothe, Florence and Lys, Michel. *Michel le jardinier au jardin de J.J. Rousseau*. Paris, 1984.

Nelli, René. *La Poésie occitane*. Paris, 1972.

Pailleux, A. and Bois, D. *Le Potager d'un curieux*. Paris, 1892; reprinted Marseilles, 1994.

Pelt, Jean-Marie. *Des Légumes*. Paris, 1993.

Phillips, Cecilia. *Letters from Provence*. London, 1975.

Pigeat, Jean-Paul. *Parcs et jardins contemporains*. Paris, 1990.

Pitte, Jean-Robert. *Histoire du paysage français*. 2 vols. Paris, 1983.

Pollan, Michael. *Second Nature*. New York, 1991.

Quintinye, Jean de la. *The Complete Gard'ner*, trans. by John Evelyn. London, 1693.

Renaud, Victor. *Les Légumes rares et oubliés*. Paris, 1991.

Richert, Alain. *Parcs et jardins extraordinaires*. Paris, n.d.

Robinson, William. *The Parks, Promenades and Gardens of Paris: Described as Considered in Relation to the Wants of Our Own Cities*. London, 1869.

Rouanet, Marie. *Tout jardin est Eden*. Marseilles, 1993.

Rousseau, Jean-Jacques. *Julie ou la Nouvelle Héloïse*. 1761. Modern edition, Paris, 1968.

Scott-James, Anne. *The Language of the Garden*. London, 1984.

——— *The Pleasure Garden*. London, 1979.

Sitwell, Edith (ed.). *A Book of Flowers*. London, 1952.

Taillemagre, Jean. *La Vie aux champs*. Paris, 1993.

Témoignages des écrivains paysans. Association Internationale des Ecrivains Paysans. Nevers, 1992.

Tournier, Michel and Herscher, Georges. *Jardins de Curé*. Arles, 1995.

Trémolet de Villers, Anne. *Trobar en Gévaudan*. Marvéjols, 1993.

Versepuy, Michel M. *Paradis terrestre: journal d'un jardin*. Paris, 1944.

Vilmorin-Andrieux. *The Vegetable Garden*, English edition published under the direction of W. Robinson. Berkeley, Calif., n.d.

Young, Arthur. *Travels in France*. London, 1792.

Index of plant names

Numerals in italics refer to captions to the illustrations.

Index of proper names

Numerals in italics refer to captions to the illustrations.

Photo credits

Frontispiece, © Robert Doisneau/Rapho.
6, 7, 12, 28, 46, 47, 58, 73, 100, 118 bottom, 138, 154, © Bibliothèque Centrale MNHN, Paris.

9, 118 top, 119, © Denis Brihat.
13, 29, 31, 47, © Roger-Viollet.
15, © Collection Viollet.
59, © Ligue Française du Coin de Terre et du Foyer.

74, © Harlingue-Viollet.
14, 72, 101, © Bibliothèque Nationale de France.
103, © Musée Goupil, Bordeaux.

DEDICATION

To Annie François, who first imagined this book...
and to the patient Cheshire Cat...

THANKS AND ACKNOWLEDGMENTS

Warm thanks to all the garden owners who took time to talk, even those who were not cited in the final version. I have never made so many new friends before in writing a single book and feel privileged to have met you all.

Warm thanks also to Marion Jablonski and Valérie Le Plouhinec for their efficiency and ever jaunty good cheer. And how to sufficiently thank Vincent Motte, with whom it is ever a privilege to work? Thanks also to our incomparable translator of the French edition, Rose-Marie Vassallo – sensitive, knowledgeable and discreet. And to Fiona Cowell who edited the American version for British readers, checking details with tact and intelligence. Thanks also to friends who advised and helped find good addresses: Georges Lévêque, Gilles Lescanff and Joëlle Mayer, Margherita Paulsen, Henri and Françoise Barberousse, Philippe Ferret, Yves Delange, Jean-Baptiste de Vilmorin, Maurice Chaudière, Peter Briggs, Catherine Curtis, Monsieur Chabrillangeas from Tulle, Monsieur Cuvelier from Fontainebleau, Pierre Lieutaghi, Alix de Saint Venant ... and many more.

And thanks also to the efficient Comités Régionaux de Tourisme who helped with the prospecting: the CRT- Nice, always so reliable, but also Poitou-Charentes, Centre Val de Loire, Normandie, Alsace, Bretagne, Midi-Pyrénées, Rhône-Alpes, Languedoc-Roussillon, and Limousin. And in particular, Marie-Yvonne Holley of the CRT-Aquitaine. No other book has brought me into contact with such a wonderful variety of people and places.

First published in Great Britain in 1997 by Thames and Hudson Ltd, London

Copyright © 1997 Editions Albin Michel S.A.

British Library Cataloguing-in-Publication Data
A catalogue record for this book is available from the British Library
ISBN 0-500-01825-1

Printed and bound in France